P9-DFO-927

RAVEN'S WIND

ALSO BY VICTOR CANNING

VICTOR CANNING

RAVEN'S WIND

William Morrow and Company, Inc.
New York   1983

Library of Congress Card Catalog Number: 83-61372

ISBN 0-688-02133-6

Printed in the United States of America

First U.S. Edition

1 2 3 4 5 6 7 8 9 10

"From the fury of the Norsemen," prayed the peasants in their churches, "good Lord deliver us!"

> "Men's cheeks faded
> On shores invaded
> When shorewards waded
>   The lords of fight;
> When monks affrighted
> To windward sighted
> The birds full-flighted
>   Of swift sea-kings;
> When churl and craven
> Saw hard on haven
> The wide-winged raven
>   At main-mast height."

(From *The Story of England* by Arthur Bryant)

1

RIADA WOKE AND lay with her eyes closed, her body lax in the aftermath of love and sleep. The warmth of the lowering, late September sun and the touch of the idle wind coming in off the sea moved over her body, caressing and waking in her the memory of the hands of Justus to whom for the first time she had gifted herself. Lying beside him, his breath coming deep and slow, she smiled to herself, knowing that left to him it would never have happened, knowing the force of his self-control, and knowing that first he would have gone to her father and mother and asked for her and would have waited until the price was paid and they had stood before the priest in the marsh chapel and God's rites had sanctified and truly ordained their union. Sweet Justus, with so much daring and craft in him and with so much reverence for the Holy Writ. Well ... God was full of forgiveness. She would confess and make penance and then the priest would join them.

She rose to her feet without disturbing him, brushed sand from her body, and then slipped her light linen smock over her head and fastened the girdle about her waist. She shook her hair to free the sun-dried sand from it and then looked down upon him. He could give two years to her own sixteen. Dark-haired, he lay partly dressed for after they had made love he had walked over to the river to pull their small fishing boat higher up the bank away from the rising tide. The crafting of huts and benches and stools was his trade, his hands, so big and awkward looking, could take a knife to soft birch wood and in a day carve and fashion it to a girdle of linked rings like the one she now wore. There was no man who could shape a coracle so swiftly and surely as he, and for the marsh

I

children he made toys which, if he had wished, he could have sold at the Lammas and other fairs for a fine profit. When they were married he would build a marsh hut for them with a carved doorway instead of a hide flap and a snug sleeping shelf to be safe against the winter floods. She knelt swiftly at his side, and kissed him on the forehead, the drop of her loose flaxen hair mingling with his raven black.

She moved away from him, taking their wicker basket to gather crab apples from a clump of trees on the landward side of the dunes. As she went in her mind was the high joy of her heart song ... a hut with a carved door and a reed-thatched roof, a hearth of baked clay, an iron cooking pot and skillet pan, and a high sleeping-place under the roof, safe from the floods, on which they could lie together in God's name and with the priest's blessing as man and wife.

Her back to the sea—autumn-misted now as the sun dropped—she walked along the twisting paths through the dunes, her feet crushing the thick-leaved sandworts. Late yellow horned-poppies still bloomed and pink and white convolvulus carpeted their landward slopes. The gentle breeze stirred the marram grasses as though a slow hand moved across them, changing their green tone from light to dark ... as she had seen the fine green stuff of the thane's lady's robe change as she moved through the great hall under the sconce lights ... rare cloth that had come with the coast-crawling traders from the South, from lands far beyond Frankland. Justus had drawn it all on a map in the sand for her once ... Justus, who from an early age had sat so many nights with Brother Eldam in his cell, learning to read and write under the one fat, draught-guttered candle. Justus's mother would have had him go for a priest but had not known, as she did, that Justus swallowed learning, the mystery of other men's trades and crafts, and the scraps of any man's experiences eagerly because he was hungry but as yet could put no name to the source or direction of his brain's questings. But priest he would never have wished for himself. He was of the world. His curiosity and his flesh denied him withdrawal from the life around him. Today proved that. Today he had become man and she woman. When they were married she would be happy to follow him wherever he led.

A hare got up from a patch of sedge ahead of her and raced away in swift zigzaggings and then stopped suddenly. It looked back at her with its long ears cocked. She laughed aloud and clapped her hands to set the beast running again.

She moved on, singing, knowing herself woman at last, the brief prelude of pain already a forgotten thing. Her mother would scold and cry and her father would beat her as a formality and that would be that. And when she carried her apples back soon to join the fish and mussels they had gathered she knew that a smile would crease Justus's broad, brown face and—she giggled to herself—she could even guess his words— *Lady, you bring the apples too late to tempt me.*

Coming to the small clump of sea-wind twisted apple trees she climbed one and, settling on a branch whose far tip held the now long-abandoned, untidy nest of a magpie, she began to fill the small straw-plaited skip she carried with the fruit. Bitter they were to the taste, but cooked and pulped and mixed with honey from her mother's hive they would make a sweet conserve to spread on the winter's flat oat-cakes.

With her basket full she rested a while on her branch. Although a light mist was gathering over the sea the air inland was clear and far away on her left hand she could see the long, smooth slopes of the Mendips.

Somewhere there Justus's married brother lived and worked at the mines for lead and tin, mines which, hundreds of years before, the Romans had opened. History to her meant nothing and time past held little curiosity for her—though when Justus told it she listened and nodded, her eyes never leaving his face, but the words slipping from her mind like water from a duck's back. And then, sometimes, he would stop in full flight, holding her eyes, and grinning would say, "Well?"

"Well, what?"

"Well, what have I been saying?"

"Does it matter? 'Tis just your face when you tell things. I could look at it forever. And when I do look I start a-dreaming."

3

And then they would fight, a rough and tumble fumbling and holding, and longing in her and mock anger in him ... until today when it had happened as she long had wanted it to happen. A spasm of remembered joy moved through her and her eyes turned to the south and west, to the flatness of the marshes, river and mere—veined and studded with the tree-topped islands of higher ground. All this was the only world she had ever known—and all this, she knew with a wisdom beyond her years, could never have held Justus to her until today. His dreams would die hard, but they would die and contentment would hold them both against all dangers and hardships until the end of their days.

She sighed and stretched her arms, feeling the quick shiver of muscle nerve between her shoulder blades. Then, eyeing the westering sun, knowing the tide had now begun to turn which would make easy their row up the river to the mere village, she knew she must get back to Justus. If she came home later than sunset her father would leather her for causing anxiety. She twisted sideways on her branch to make ready to drop to the ground one-handed while in the other hand she held her full basket. She stopped suddenly as her face turned seawards.

Beyond the last of the seaward dunes she could see the slow break of a gentle swell against the long beach and the broadening waters of the river where it met the sea and the incoming tide and then beyond, a low curtain of sea mist gently creeping landwards on the southerly wind. Her eyes marked at once the slow, ghost-like slide through the mist of first undetailed mass and then within seconds the rise and fall of oars and the water scurry they made. Out of the mist as though it were a true beast, many legged, eager for land and ravaging, the dragon's head at the prow dipping and rising on swell and oar thrusts came the sea raiders' craft. Its great square sail was dropped and furled and lay stowed between the starboard and port rowers. It came in swiftly, the high bow creaming the sea along its flanks. A few times before she had seen such ships pass distantly along the coast for they never stopped to raid here where cattle were few, rich plunder absent, and the marsh ways too dangerous to try without a reliable guide.

4

Frantically she began to shout to warn Justus if he should still be sleeping, but the wind in her face and the breaking waves on the pebble strand swamped her calls. For a moment or two she was tempted to drop to the ground and run for the beach. Then she knew she could never reach it in time. She shut her eyes, crossed herself, and prayed to the Holy Mother that Justus would have wakened by now and had seen the dragon craft coming. If he had his feet would save him. Two bow shots away lay the beginning of the marshes and once that was reached they would both be safe. By taking hidden pathways and swimming like otters they would swiftly lose the pursuing sea pirates. She opened her eyes, searching the dune paths for sight of the running Justus, ready to meet and run with him. But there was no sign of him and as she watched she saw the dragon ship ride the last breakers into the beach, running high on to it from the thrust of oars and the following sea. The oars were shipped and men leaped overboard on either side and ran the craft well up the strand where it rested, its stern rising and falling rhythmically as the breaking swell ran past it. Realizing then that she might be seen in the tree, she dropped to the ground, abandoned her basket and apples, and ran to the landward side of a high dune where, hidden by a growth of wind-shaped tamarisk, she watched the beach and began to pray ... *Holy Mary, Mother of the Holy Babe ... let Justus be awake ... Let Justus be awake ...*

*　　*　　*　　*

But Justus was not awake. Night to him was as familiar as day, and a man worked and hunted as the seasons and the night and day demanded. Sleep was something you bowed to when the body would no longer be denied its relief. Last evening, after he had finished crafting in his workshed, he had had a quick bowl of soup and half of a cold roast mallard he had taken in his duck trap, kissed his widowed mother goodnight and had gone out to set his eel traps afresh, for they were running now for the sea. Then he had gone up river to the otter pool. Spring cubs were now near full growth and the

5

families were broken up. By the last full moon before Michael-mas they were away on their own and still far from having the wisdom of their parents. He had tied a freshly caught roach by its tail to a hazel wand and set it so that it swung free and just out of reach over the mere pool bank and then had sat out of the moonlight in a patch of reed mace with his bow, the arrow notched and ready to be drawn and loosed, waiting—as he had told himself—for curiosity to kill the otter. He had waited two hours, eyes and ears alert to all the night sounds and sights before an otter had come, and knowing it had come before he saw it for its taint came downwind and to him. When the otter slid out under the star and now waning moonlight, he shot it through the skull as it stood on the bank raising its muzzle to the smell of the fish so tantalizingly distant. He had pouched it in his hunting sack, and an hour later had shot another. He had been well pleased with himself, for at Michaelmas Buic, his thane, had promised him a silver arm ring if he brought enough pelts to make a good riding winter cloak for his wife before the bad weather set in ... Then, the next morning, Riada with her blue eyes and golden hair had come and teased and cajoled him to take her down the river to the sea to gather shellfish ...

So now, from lack of sleep and the langour of true first loving, he lay flat on his back, naked except for his knee-length skin trews, his head cushioned on his piled tunic while his spirit roamed happily in some dream world. At his feet stood Noth, warrior, master shipwright and steersman from the Danish war-craft which rested partly beached at the water's edge. Four crewmen stood with Noth, leather-helmeted for sea work, rough linen sailing smocks falling to their knees, sword-belted and armed for coming ashore. Each man carried a goatskin water bag. And each man waited for Noth to give them the sign. Only one man stood above Noth and that was their lord Oric of Gerskat and he was now crouching at the water's edge not far from the war-craft, easing his bowels against an attack of wine looseness.

Noth looked down at the youth. He had had a son once who had died when he was in early manhood. The memory

6

held him now—as it had often done in the past—and prompted him to a faint stir of compassion. Normally they would have sliced the youth's bare torso with a sword so that the guts tumbled out like red corn from a split sack and he would have gone to—with luck—the Christian heaven and the Jesus father God which these Saxons had turned to when they had taken his land. But now he weighed sentiment against need. By battle and sickness they were short-handed. Bad luck had dogged them, and worse weather crossed them. They still had the long haul to make. West and about the end of this land and then the long run eastwards past Wight and Thanet and into their own North Sea. Against thirst with undrinkable water as far as the eyes could reach a man could suck pebbles, and against hunger . . . well, it would not be the first time he had chewed away the overlap of his leather sword belt. But now the spilt guts of a Saxon on the sand would be a waste. A young man's muscled arms and shoulders were a gift from the gods.

Quietly he said, "He comes with us to sit on a thwart and row when the wind fails. Do him no harm." With a nod to two of his men to take the youth, he beckoned the others to follow him and, without a backward glance, began to walk across the high water tide-wrack towards the river mouth where he had seen Justus's marsh boat drawn up clear of the water.

When they came to it they found inside a flat bowled rush basket covered with seaweed to protect its contents from the sun. Oricson, the eldest son of their chief—who could claim only a few more years than the prisoner they had taken and for whom this was his first Raven voyage—pulled the covering from the bowl. Inside lay a heap of shell fish—mussels and cockles that would make fine sea soup—and a score of small dabfish, each bearing on its back the mark of the fish spear which lay alongside the basket. Wrapped in a cloth was half the remains of a large hard-tack barley loaf.

Looking at Noth, Oricson said, "Not much, Noth. But enough to make a good sea-soup. My belly grumbles for better commons. Should we not go inland a bit and try for some churl's cow or goat?"

7

For a moment or two Noth made no answer. He was looking at the boat. It was a spear and a half in length, the bow pointed, its lines running back to broaden amidships and then keeping those lines to its square stern. Two short oak oars lay along its floor boards and its frame covering was of thick hides, each neatly overlapped and stitched with gut to the other, cut and shaped to fit the curve of the framework. Master shipwright himself, he could fault it here and there. Not stable enough for work in a rough sea, but more than adequate for marsh and river work and as distant as Valhalla from Hades compared with the rough coracles most of the marsh men used.

Absently he said, "We cook and eat what we have and go. A fish soup will fill our bellies' bilges and keep us going until we can find better pickings. Bring the boat. Since we have lost our own we can use it."

Oricson smiled. "Sweet Noth—your eyes have the women-want look in them. For this—some web-footed marshman's craft?"

Noth, unpiqued, said easily, "Women cook and weave, are bundled on the sleeping benches and, in my day, I have filled them with named and un-named children. That trade is common to all men. But only to some men do the gods give high gifts of craft. Bring the boat—we need it—especially since it was you that lost our own on the Irish rocks by over-loading it with spoils. But do not frown. It has happened to others and will happen again."

They trudged back across the sands to their companions, dragging the boat which held their meagre spoils between them. The others had lit a fire over which hung their cooking pot in which stewed the meagre last of the horse flesh from the carcass they had carried with them from their unhappy Irish venture. Into the pot went their find of shellfish and dabs. At hand lay their weapons and one man, bowl in his palm full of the cauldron stew, went off to the nearest dune top to keep watch. Behind them their dragon craft rose and fell on the easy swell, held by an anchor streamed from the stern, its high bows just nudging the shore and moving gently in with the coming of the tide.

8

Noth sat apart with Oric, both cradling their eating bowls and spooning out the fish and flesh soup. Oric, tall and broad-shouldered, over forty winters showing in the whitening of his blond hair and on the long, lean hard-bitten face with a scar mark that ran from the left corner of his mouth like a white, never browning chalkmark to below his left ear, grinned at Noth. "The gods were charitable. Small dole they give us this year so far. But for a marsh lad's pickings I give thanks."

"He's aboard?"

"Trussed and bound like a Saxon sausage." He grinned. "Perhaps we should eat him instead of putting him on a rowing bench?"

"Should that be so then I think the gods would try us hard on the voyage home."

"How so?"

"I think they may have gifted us." Noth nodded to the small boat which lay on the sands beyond the cooking fire. "I think he made that. If he did then one of his gods must have gifted him too. If he did—then I want him. I grow old and there is no one at Gerskat who can truly follow me when I am gone. You have had me to serve you. Who shall serve Oricson? If he is what I think he is gift him to me and I ask no share of the plunder from this raiding season."

Oric laughed, spat a fish bone to the sand, and said, "What plunder? Not even a bag of pearls for my wife to string for her neck, nor abbey gold and silver plate for the smith to work into fine jewellery for her. Such a homecoming—she will turn her back on me in the wall bed—not that that can be any woman's final answer. Anyhow ... we will see. When we go east about this land's end the gods may favour us with rich pickings from the Devon men and the West Saxons—from the Cornish you can expect nothing except scraggy cattle and fluke-ridden sheep. By Odin's raven, never have I known such a season ... and now Oricson itches to be away next year to try his fortune with the Grand Army."

"Make me the gifting I ask."

Oric scratched his chin, and rubbed soup slop from his salt

and wind-cracked lips, and then said, "If all be well and things are with the lad as you imagine, I will. If not I sell him as slave. We need no more mouths to feed this winter. But be warned Noth—you are always three jumps ahead of everyone else with your plans. And how often at the last jump have you gone into the pig mire up to your waist? The boy may have stolen or borrowed the boat. These marsh folk have nothing. It is said that even the old Romans left them alone. Not worth the life of a single man for the pickings or talents they offered."

*　　*　　*　　*

Justus lay on the stern boards close under the feet of the steersman who manned the heavy rudder oar that hung over the starboard side. The steersman sat perched above him, half-leaning on the rudder shaft, his eyes going now and again to the great sail which had been hoisted to catch a rising night breeze. None of the crew rowed now. They all slept except for a watch at the bows and a man amidship of the stout mast who under Noth's orders waited to keep the great sail trimmed fairly before the wind. Though there was no need much for it since the wind was steady and not strong enough to send any bow spray back over the boat. Now and again he saw the steersman's eyes go from the moon in her last quarter and then to the pole star as the ship moved westwards some miles off the Cornish coast ... his own marshlands already left far behind on the port side. The rest of the crew slept hard on the deck boards, their shields all inboard and packed with rough sacking for pillows, their bodies rolled in blankets. Some snored like pigs, some talked in their sleep, and once a man shouted a loud war cry as his dream took him back into battle. They were hard men and well used to rough lying.

Misery inhabited him like a belly wound, and recent memories flashed through his mind with a colour and a passion which brought gall into his throat and made him grind his teeth in bitter anger. There had been a love-gifting of bodies between himself and Riada and there would have followed holy marriage. No other maiden lived for him. It was small sin, and common enough among his people, but God, swift to anger, had not stayed his punishment. Though, by the Holy Saints, he could not help but find it over-pushed for a weakness that Adam and millions of other men had shared. Against Riada there was no anger or bitterness. Long distant Eve had mothered her and she but shared what all women had inherited unless they were saints. Only one gift from the Almighty gave him ease—that Riada had not lain sleeping with him when the Dane men had come for if she had she would have been lying now on the far beach, ravished in turn by every crew man and then left under the night stars, spatchcocked from breasts to groin, naked for the first foxes or wolves to find her. *Dear Holy Mother of Jesus, Sainted Mary, for that charity be forever praised.*

He stirred against the bite of the bonds that held his arms behind him and his ankles tight-bound. Slop water from the ship's run had soaked into his clothes and even in his misery he thought that if he were master the man on the watch at the mast should have been put to work with a baling pan. There was more than slop-water washing in the bilge. Somewhere a hull plank had sprung. He groaned a little, his nature betrayed briefly by his misery. Hardship was nothing. The whole world lived or died by it.

Almost above him the helmsman leaned forward a little and called to the man on watch under the mainmast. At that moment the words meant nothing to Justus, but from the angle at which he was lying he saw the man move slightly amidships, heard the noise of a grating being lifted and a few moments later the sound of water being baled from the bottom boards and flung overboard. For a moment or two he had the odd thought that the man had read his mind's working. Among many others, strange tales were told of these Danemark men ... that they had second sight that saw with clarity as coloured as any picture in a monk's missal the coming of the future. That they went into battle knowing whether they would live or die ... that they could close their eyes and see the weather ahead for days ... that they could look at the night stars and divine in the desolation of the sea how many days it would be before they sighted land, and that they had a certainty of life after death which made the thin faith of many a good Christian shamed.

Behind him the helmsman said something in a quiet voice. The words escaped him in meaning though some dim recognition tantalized his mind. The man spoke again slowly and spacing his words, and this time he mostly understood them for it was his own language with a strangeness that held no bar if one listened carefully—and then, even in his misery, he knew why not. His father was of Saxon blood—though his mother was a marsh woman of British blood and speech. And Saxon mother speech, his marsh priest had told him, was related to the Danish since that country and Old Saxony lay side by side across the North Sea.

The man repeated his words again, even more slowly, and this time they came intelligibly enough to him.

"What is your name?"

He screwed his head around to look at the helmsman, perched above him, the butt of the steering oar tucked under his arm while his other cradled a small wine skin to his belly.

He said, "Justus."

"No more than that?"

"Justus the son of Anac, late huntsman to the Thane of Parretmoor."

"You would drink?" The man tapped the wineskin and without waiting for a reply, went on, "I am Noth of Gerskat. That is in Danemark. You would drink?"

Almost without his volition Justus nodded. Noth let the rudder run free and bent down and with both hands held the wine skin to the youth's mouth and said, "There is little left. Finish it. If the others knew I still had it ..." he laughed, "... they might have been tempted to cut my throat for it."

Justus drank briefly and then as Noth tipped the skin finished the little that was in it. He had never drunk wine before and knew nothing about it, but it pleased him with its taste and he could feel it spread a fierce fire through his cramped and cold body.

Noth said, "It is as good a thing as we ever—more's the pity—got out of Ireland this season. They call it *uisgebeatha* which means life-water. The crew swilled it like pigs and for a day lay so drunk on the beach that a handful of women with bodkins could have massacred the lot. Like all good things—unless it's a due feast sanctioned by the gods—it should be taken in moderation. So . . . Justus, you fall asleep on a beach, and your gods fail you."

"There is only one God."

"Ah . . . yes, that you believe, I know. Well, we will not quarrel about gods. They can be left to do that by themselves. At the moment I would talk about you."

"I could talk easier if my hands were free so that I could sit with some ease."

Noth laughed. "Some time later, perhaps. We are only a few miles off shore. One like you could keep afloat just with hands and arms and I'm sure you know each set and turn of the tides and the currents to help you."

"Why should I?"

"The gods tell me so. And my eyes tell me that you are one who lacks no courage or self-wisdom. Be content a little. The snow falls and one day it melts. The floods rise but in the end they drop. Unwisely you slept today and let us take you. Maybe it was the unwisdom of a lifetime. Maybe your God marked you for this day."

"You talk in riddles."

"No. I have eyes—and I know when to keep my tongue bridled. The sand alongside you as you slept had also been the resting place of someone else. And as we brought your boat back from the river she was watching safely from a far dune. Though I doubt whether she could be caught our men will take a chance for any woman—so I said nothing."

"I thank you for that."

"The time may come when you will thank me for other things. Without me you would be lying spatchcocked on the sands. But you are here—and your boat."

"Why the boat?"

"Did you fashion it?"

13

"Yes."

"Then that is why."

"You riddle me."

"Not for long. And if in the days to come we treat you harshly in body believe me there is more gain in being alive than left dead for the foxes and the eagles on a marshland shore. Now—" Noth pulled a heavy wool cloak from behind him and spread it over Justus. "Sleep if you can. You belong to me. Slave if you like to begin with—but with the grace of the gods time may make you feel more like a son. But if not that, a man of gratitude because you are still living which in its way is not an entirely unpleasant state for any man no matter what griefs he nurses. Grief passes. No man can escape that change because it is the life tide of the human spirit. Now sleep if you can."

*　　*　　*　　*

When Riada arrived home near midnight, having had to walk the devious and roundabout marsh paths instead of coming back up river, her father, always hasty of temper, began to give her a beating but after a few blows his wife Larna, stepped forward and held his arm, saying, "You waste your anger on someone who feels nothing, Pendar. More sense is to ask her where is Justus. Had he kept her late he would have been man enough to bring her to us."

Pendar shook her arm from him. "Man enough! Is that not plain to guess? He has been man enough to man her and not man enough to stay with her. Come day, and I will deal with him."

"Maybe so—but let the girl speak. The beating will keep if there be need for it." Larna looked down at Riada sitting on the edge of the narrow bedshelf and said gently, "Come child—tell us what has happened."

For a moment or two Riada said nothing. Then looking up at them, her mud-caked and thorn-torn hands cupped about her cheeks, began to tell them in a toneless, flat voice all that had happened. Deliberately, because in her heart she knew

14

that she would never see Justus again, she told the whole plain truth of their loving and the arrival of the longship and Justus's capture and how she had seen him taken away with the sea pirates, and of the hours she had spent making her way back from the sea dunes. As she spoke her mind cleared and her spirit turned from her grief into a clear-sighted, practical acceptance of the change the Fates had forced on her life. She would never see Justus again. He was gone into slavery or, perhaps, death at sea. Now, and for a long time to come, she would carry her mourning until one day the ache would cease and memory would mist into the near peace of accepting God's will and purpose. Even now there was an acceptance in her of the sharp justice which had been doomed for her.

She said boldly, "There was loving between us for the first time. You may beat me when I say I hope there will be a fruit-ing of our love. It is for you now to choose me a man. With Justus gone all men are the same. Whatever man you find for me—he shall know the truth. But now—" She stood up slowly and straightened her long slim body, bracing her shoulders a little with the onset of a new spirit, and said, "—I shall go now and tell Justus's widowed mother this sad day's tale, and shall stay with her until morning. And, father, this I say—choose whom you will for me, but if once again you lay the ash plant to my shoulders I shall leave this place and go find some service in hall or nunnery far from here."

Her father stirred angrily, but the touch of his wife's hand on his arm held back his ire. Then with a shrug of his shoulders he said calmly, "Your place is here in the marshlands. To-morrow I will speak for you with one who will willingly accept all that has been, and take you to wife gladly. I talk of Arnulf, the mason, who lost his wife in the Spring fever and has now come back from Glastonbury. Since he travels much to his work you will go with him and be a good wife to him." He paused a little and then went on, his voice gentler, faintly touched with compassion, "He will treat you well and honestly."

When she had gone he went to the rushlight burning on

the centre post of the hut and trimmed its stiff wick with a snap of his fingers and without turning said, "I would have had Justus for her. But the gods have taken him. I pray that they stand by him."

"The gods?"

"Aye, the gods. No matter what the monks say. You think only one God can shape and turn the lives of all men? There is in my mind a God of gods and then the men here on earth who are marked as his saints. And sometimes they let the reins of all their charges get tangled between their many fingers."

"Say that to the bishop's face and you know what to expect."

"The bishop! I could tell you things about the bishop at the hunting feasts which would shame you."

*　　*　　*　　*

With the coming of morning the easterly wind before which they had been running all night died away. Land lay away on their port bow, distantly seen through a light haze. They hove-to and the crew ate quickly of the cold commons they had aboard and relieved themselves in turn over the side of the ship and then washed themselves and any foulness which had marked the outer strake boards of the long hull. Justus's hands and feet were untied so that he might do the same, but Oricson, grinning, slipped a rope nose round his neck and said, "Jump Saxon, if you wish to meet two deaths where most men are content with one—throttling and drowning. Be content to ease your bowels—for that is the way good Noth wishes it."

With the great square mainsail dropped and furled for want of wind the oars were manned. Normally the ship had place for eighteen oarsmen, but now from their losses of men only thirteen oars were manned. Oric, coming aft from the bows to the stern where Noth stood at the steering oar, looked down at Justus who had been fully bound again and then said to Noth, "We need another man at the oars. He's strong. We could use him. You think you can keep him trussed there like a roll of fine abbey tapestry for the rest of our time at sea?"

"The wild falcon must be gentled before you can trust him. Give him a few more days to take the heart from him and you shall have him at the oars."

"He could be there now—with Oricson behind him with a stabbing knife resting to hand."

"He might take that chance while we follow the coast closely. When we have rounded this land's end and can stand out to sea you will have no trouble with him. This I promise. But if I am proved wrong—remember you have gifted him to me so the loss will be mine. One loss already I have suffered when the marsh fever took my son last year. You have seen this Saxon's boat—the gods have gifted his hands and given him the brains to use them. Be patient, my chief—and you will take profit from it."

"So be it—but he is your charge."

"My thanks. Odin gave one eye for the gift of understanding. You have it—and yet see with both."

Oric, standing easy to the roll and surge of the craft under the oars, laughed and spat to leeward and said, "You talk now as you used when we were young to talk to a woman to charm her into taking a soft fall. Talk sometime to Oricson and charm him from his lust to join the Grand Army."

Noth shook his head. "No. One day he will go. There is no bridling his dream. And you have other sons ... aye, and will have more if you make the right offerings to Frey and Freya."

Oric went forward and took his place among the rowers. Justus watched him go and watched, too, the skilled work of these men with their oars, feeling the craft lift with the power of their sweeps, hearing the sea song of the water below the hull and feeling in himself, sharp across his contained misery, the thin edge of pleasure at their skill and their shipcrafting which had made them the dreaded sea pirates they were.

Behind him Noth said, "You understood the talk?"

"Enough."

"You want to live?"

"Who does not?"

"Many—when the berserk madness takes them. But the gods made such men deliberately. Odin gave one eye willingly to gain the gift of understanding and wisdom. In a lesser way some men are gifted from birth with different kinds of understanding. I think you are one."

"Why?"

"By answering a first question you will prove me right."

"Ask it."

"I will. Your people move about the marsh waters and meres using clumsy coracles. But you ... you fashioned for yourself that craft forward. Why?"

Justus was silent for a while and then said, "Because a coracle is an unbroken pony. It obeys no will but its own ... oh, in time you get to know its way but never to trust it. I made my boat because it does what I want to—it moves as a fish does, as a bird flies, and with touch answers a true command instead of wanting always to be a whirligig water beetle."

Noth laughed, and then said, "Be patient. The gods have changed your destiny. Your God or the gods—it matters not which. I promise you that, when we round this land's end, you shall have more freedom whenever we are running far from land. I had a son—and he has gone. Son I can never call you. But I would treat you like one and teach you my craft. Your West Saxon country you will never see again—but a wise man learns to live with any change in life."

"With slavery?"

"There will be no slavery for you. I will swear a bond oath for you and you will be mine until the day I die. And you will swear on your Holy Jesus and His Holy Father to abide by that oath until I am dead."

"And after that?"

"All oaths die with me. But by then you will have married one of our girls, had children, and grown rich at my craft— and there will be nothing to draw you back to this land."

*   *   *   *

18

The next morning long before sunrise the Danes ran their ship into a steep-sided Cornish cove with a scattering of huts and byres on the foot of the heather and grass slope which ran up to the moorlands beyond. A war-band of the Danes, leather-helmeted and jerkined, carrying short, broad-bladed swords and sharp pointed scramaseax daggers, dropped into the shallow water and waded ashore while Noth swung the long ship's bows round to meet the incoming swell and two oarsman a side kept her headed up to the seas, holding her there while they waited for the raiding party to return.

Long before the raiding party reached the first of the huts men, women and children were in flight up the steep slope of the cliff combe, carrying what they could of their possessions and driving a few hastily herded cattle before them. No man turned to offer fight. They fled in a rabble, leaving behind them those too old or too sick to run.

Squatting near Noth in the stern of the *Fafnir* Justus watched with a sick and angry heart as the first screams of the helpless in the huts rose into the clear September air. In a little while the first of the poor huts was ablaze from the thatch brands the Danes lit from the cooking fires. One by one the huts blazed and clear above the call of the high circling seabirds and the screams of the burning aged and helpless came the wild berserk chant of the *Fafnir*'s raiding party as they rampaged and murdered, tore the small cattle pens apart and slew all the sheep, heedless of the fact that there were more than they could possibly bring back for the ship's provisioning.

Hardly aware that he said it, he was so sick at heart, Justus turned to Noth angrily and shouted, "These are not men— they are devils!"

His face solemn as a mask for his own emotions Noth replied, "When the thatch blooms like a red flower with flames, and the dying scream, that is warmth and music to men long at sea since the only world they know and love has become this *Fafnir*. *Fafnir* the Dragon drives them. But when we are back beached on the home strand then you will see that they become men again, gentle with their wives and children, tender lovers and good husbandry men. And remember this for your own life's sake—you may say such things to me, but keep your lips oyster-shut before the crew for, if you cross one while he nurses the madness of berserk, his sword will rip your guts and neither I nor Oric, nor any other man could save you." He was silent for a while as the breaking surge chanted on the shore and the screams and shouts from the village filled the air and the gulls and prey birds chorused shrilly overhead. Then with a wry twist of his brown, lined face, he went on, "And mark this—before the day is out you will eat the provender they bring back ... aye and drink the poor barley beer and wort-berry wine that comes aboard with them. If you would live—then you must accept what men are. You have a good understanding. Let it control you words and your body."

Words which were true for that evening at full tide they beached the *Fafnir* at high water on the sands of a small island a half day's sailing from the village they had pillaged and there they built a driftwood fire and roasted their sheep meat and ate fully. They filled their brine tubs to the full to pickle against lean days. They drank their barley beer and wort-berry wine of which there was not so much that the crew got drunk and quarrelsome, but it put some fire into their veins and they sat late under the stars and sang their skaldic songs led by Oricson, who had a fine, strong voice.

Wrist and ankle bound after eating Justus lay in the firelight, his face turned to the sea, and listened to the songs and the occasional outbreaks of drink-stirred banter and quarrel.

He was beginning now to have the ear for their speech and to recognize in some strange word suddenly the ghost of his own Saxon word which lay behind it.

> *... with sword and spear*
> *slippery with bright blood*
> *where kites wheeled. And how well*
> *we violent sea-swords clashed!*
> *Kingfisher flames ate up hut roofs*
> *Raging we killed and killed and*
> *Skewered bodies lay, death sleeping,*
> *In the great town's portway ...*

He turned away on his side to watch the starlight reflection on the wet tide-free sands. Misery took his body like an ague and there was darkness in his thoughts that made him feel that, if ever the chance came, bound or unbound, a thousand leagues of sea between him and any land, he would go over the freeboard and let God guide his destiny—for even death surely must be more welcome than anything that lay before him. Death would be more honourable than to go meekly into bondage—no matter Noth's kindness and promises. And then, as it had before, came the sharp bite of bitterness as he thought of Riada. God, he had thought more than once since his taking, had made her wake and stray into the dunes to safety. For that he praised God. She would never see him again. Slowly with the passing of the days the heart ache would ease and she would—even as if he had stepped stupidly into quick quagmire on the marshes and been swallowed from sight—wrap her sorrow with a passing of days and weeks and months and come finally out into the sunlight of life again. Maybe, if he lived, that would happen for him, too. Man must live in the present. The past was a fallen leaf that, sered, was blown by the winds and powdered into nothingness.

Behind him suddenly two Danes began to quarrel and shout and then to fight and he heard the stamp of their fellows' feet and their calls of encouragement and derision. Then slowly Justus rolled on to his side so that his face was hidden from the firelight. With no noise, no movement of his body or limbs, his eyes fixed on the phosphorescent wave break over the strand, he began to weep so that sea gleams and star glow danced and sparked in a mazy motion and the tension of his body muscles gripped him more rigidly than any of his bonds.

When the weakness of spirit had left him he knew that it could never come again to him. He was shrived of self-pity. God in His wisdom had set his destiny along strange ways. Acceptance was no weakness, only an embracing of God's will.

*   *   *   *

Arnulf the stone-mason and Riada sat in the noon sun beneath the high elms that crowned the crest of the Island of Athelings. Below them an early mist hid the river and the marsh meres. But up here sunlight held the land and corn-crakes called from the strip crops of barley and oats which marked its southern slopes. Arnulf was a small, thick-set man who had known well over twice the years which Riada had lived. His rough hands were callused from his craft and his face lined and wind and weather roughened. His eyes were as blue as periwinkle, clear, and wrinkled deeply at their corners. But as he sat now and his hands worked at the purple-vetch flowers which she had gathered as they climbed the rise Riada recognized the fineness of his stubby fingers' mastery of their stems and blooms. An ugly man, but honest and kind, as she knew from repute. He was a man of worth for he had more calls from minster and abbey than he could meet; and since he mixed with men of learning, men who could read and write the Roman Latin language, men with the gift in their hands to colour the pages of their Holy books with the strange beasts and jewel-like flowers and patterns, she knew that all the world would think that he did her honour by asking for her in marriage, to take her, and to bed her and bring into the world children ... all things she had looked one day to share with Justus. There would be no hardship in being wife to him. But never in the innermost of her mind would there ever depart her love for Justus—though now, since common-sense had not deserted her in grief or despair, she knew that Justus was gone for ever.

Arnulf said, "In a week I go to Exeter to work for the Bishop there. I shall be there for many weeks. It is a year now since my wife died. When work is done at the end of a day and a man is alone it is good to come back and grumble to someone about rotten stone and clumsy workmen. To some-one whose face, when I carve the capital of a pillar, I put among the figures of angels in the frieze and so know that for a thousand years and more she will be there. That secret is one to be shared. I would share it with you. I am not entirely a good man ... when I trace a design first in the sand or on a slate and it goes wrong I shout at any whose shadow passes. On feast days I drink too much sometimes and if crossed will throw tainted or badly cooked meat into the fire. But never in the whole of my life have I raised my hand to a woman ... Holy Mary, no. God made them for cherishing." Gently he placed the circlet of vetch flowers on her head.

Despite herself Riada laughed and said, "Are you taking the long road instead of the short to ask me whether I would go to Exeter with you?"

"As my wife, yes. But know this. Justus is in your heart and will rest there till God's kindness dims the memory. Only when you say so will we bed together."

"You know that there may be a child of his that I begin to carry?"

"Then that child shall be as mine. And then ..." he chuckled, "... there shall follow ours. But the first born shall be the first born. And if he has the hands and eyes I will raise him in my craft, and, who knows, when the time comes that he is man he will be called to Winchester from the fame of his craft to work for one of the Kings of the House of Cerdic? And there, maybe, he will do such work to God's glory that will outlive all the following kings of this land." He paused briefly and then excitedly cried out, boyishly, "Oh, yes ... Oh, yes ... Good stone and great craft outlive a thousand kings. And—" He broke off suddenly.

"Something ails you?"

He shook his head. "I know not. I speak to you only as I talk to myself when I work alone high on the scaffolding runs because I am happy at the hope which wakes in my heart and so—may God forgive me—I forget your still undried grief."

She said, "You talk of work to the glory of God for a future son. Our son. It is talk that is sensible and begins to take a woman the first way along the path that leads to the acceptance of God's will. I will come with you and be a good wife."

Arnulf stood up, took her hand and raised her to stand with him and said, "I will take you back now and for the comfort of both of us you will sleep a week of nights on all this, and then

23

I will come to you for your answer which I shall know by one look at your face." He grinned unexpectedly, and went on, "I should tell you one other thing."

"And that?"

"Because of my work I wash my whole body every night. But since a man cannot reach his own back you would have to—"

"My answer is and always will be yes to your commands. The cock rules the roost. There is no going against Nature. Justus once said—" she broke off sharply.

For a moment or two Arnulf was silent. Then he took her arm and began to walk her down the slope, through the fox-glove spikes already crested with greening seed capsules and the high grasses which powdered their clothes with pollen.

Arnulf said tenderly, "Give time its run and grief its term. God renews the broken spirit."

* * * *

Three days later they rounded the far western point of the land's end, giving it a wide berth and setting an easterly course. There were times when, with the tide beneath them and favoured by a westerly wind, the *Fafnir* ran free under her sail and there was long rest for the oarsmen. At other times the slack sail was dropped and the long sweeps came out and the Danes, split into sea watches, drove the warcraft up channel, taking the sea spume and flying spray on their backs with complete indifference, and now Justus worked with them and in the same watch as Oricson, who manned the next oar forward of him. Oricson had become his keeper. They freed his wrist and arm bindings when he rowed but his legs were slightly hobbled from ankle to ankle. Around his waist was a thick hide rope that ran behind him to a spare anchor which lay at Oricson's feet.

On his first full watch as the *Fafnir* headed eastwards Oricson had said pleasantly, "Only the gods can do the impossible. I have heard said that once two bog Irish Christian priests floated from their land to yours on a mill-

24

stone. Your priests, though, are mad liars. I like you fair enough but if you make one wrong move—then my sea-dagger will be in your back. Noth would not want that to happen."

"I'm no fool."

"Aye, that begins to show—for already you handle the long oar with some niceness. Noth has claimed you and nobody in sober mind ever gainsays Noth—so forget wild thoughts, Saxon."

"And if you were sitting in my place, would you forget yours?"

"Ah, you listen to crew gossip. But there is no wildness in wanting to join the Grand Army. What we do here with my father is no more than mice nibbling at the corner of a barley sack. It has always been that way with him—and I put no blame to him for that. But bigger prizes wait for the bold. Next year it is told that the Great Army will come to your land—and come to stay. And by Thor I mean to be with it, fighting in the warbands of Ivor the Boneless and Halfdan, sons of the great Ragnar Lothbroke. We shall take the land and hold it and your people will be our serfs."

"The Roman legions came and went."

"Then we shall do what the Romans never could ..."

"Why should you want to leave your own lands?"

Oricson laughed. "The winter nights are long. We breed too fast and the land cannot take our weight. You Saxons—near neighbours once—did the same thing long ago."

"I am no Saxon. I am a marshman, and my people were in the marshes long before the Romans came. But I am a good subject of King Ethelred of the West Saxons."

"Is it true that some marsh people are web-footed? Aye ... now that would be something to sing of in hall, of taking a web-footed marsh girl. Tell me, do some of them even have scales on their backsides ... ?" Oricson roared aloud with laughter at his own wit.

Sharply Justus said, "And is it true that ..." He broke off, killing the words which were about to come from his mouth.

Oricson's voice came menacingly from behind him. "Say on, web-foot, say on."

"Not this time. But one day, if I ever stand free man again and we face one another armed, I will say it."

There was silence from Oricson for a while. The long oars dipped and swung, and the trodden sea sang under the keel of the *Fafnir*. Then he said calmly, "I like you well for your spirit. But you escape with an easy promise. But should the gods prove me wrong—when that day comes, I will give you your say and then slit your guts free of your body. But until then know that I mark you as I mark myself—easy in friendship, and bloody in anger."

"Your words are fair. The future rests with God."

"The gods."

"Say it as you will—and I will do the same."

That night as Justus lay close to the small steering platform in the stern, wrapped in an old sailing tunic Noth had given him, his wrists bound and his legs shackled with skin thongs to a spare anchor, Noth came aft to take his turn at the steering oar. The wind was fair and steady and the night clear and most of the crew—since the great square sail had been hoisted —slept like wrapped corpses on the boards, their heads cushioned in the padded hollows of their shields which were all inboard while the *Fafnir* held steady to a long sea course.

After a while Noth said, "So you have become friends with Oricson, and each sworn to kill the other should you ever meet as freemen."

"There was talk that way."

"A strange friendship. But I say no more. Youth blood is hot and heats the brain so that the young find strange and rash words escaping from their mouths. For your part I give you now a fair warning. You have my protection—but in anger there are those who will give that no thought. I would do all I can for you except give you true freedom and a return to your country. Accept this. It is better to live with an itch you can scratch than to die for a few angry words provoked by some young fool over-eager to prove his manhood. Take what I say to heart."

Justus was silent for a while. Nothing he knew could ever quell the longing in him sometime and somehow to return

26

to his country. But Noth spoke sense. It was better to live with hope, than to die for some passing spleen at a drunken insult.

He said, "What you say is true. I take it to heart and will begin to live by it."

Noth gave a quiet chuckle. "Now you begin to be gentled. I take your word and so give you back some of your freedom. After tonight you shall move freely and work so at the oars. Only when we move to shore will you be bound."

"Why do you say after tonight?"

"Because now we run close to land, and the tide sets that way towards the Wessex coast."

"How can you know this?"

"Could you take your boat on a night of cloud darkness through your marsh meres and channels?"

"I could."

"How could you?"

"I know not."

"'Tis no mystery. Within every man if he gives it room to live is another man who is guided by a wisdom that comes from the gods. A prince can walk through his night dark palace without stumbling, one of your monks through the bat-light of a monastery with sure feet to take him to the altar ... aye, and a villain step his way unheard across the darkness of a great hall, where his warrior comrades snore in the straw, to do some mischief."

"And it is in this way that you can sit there and hold the *Fafnir* on a true course?"

"Aye, but do not ask me how—except that I know always where the Pole Star stands without seeing it. That a wind that comes in over leagues of open sea has a smell which is sharper and different from a land wind. If a man were to move to his bed in darkness and the woman waiting there were not his wife—do you think he would not know the difference when he took her in his arms? How think you that the wild geese come each winter from the Tartary lands to our coasts, or that the swallows each spring come swinging north from the far south Moorish lands?" He laughed. "Mind you, it is always

27

a comfort when the eyes can prove the brain's wisdom, for in a man it is less sharp than in animals for once the gods made all living things pure and endowed with their own destinies— but man was marred by his own greed since in every man's heart is a wish to be a god. And that can never be. Now sleep and be wise."

Justus rolled over to find fresh body comfort and shut his eyes. But sleep he knew would be long a-coming to him. Noth's words hung in his mind and he accepted their wisdom. Christ had died on the cross for mankind. Each man should honour that martyrdom and know that in human suffering there could never be more than the pale shadow of His great sacrifice for man.

The next day when he took his place with the oars Oricson, seeing his free state, gave a little laugh and said, "So, good Noth has given the marshman his freedom, and the marshman has given his word. Had our places been changed no Saxon would have drawn such a word giving from me."

Justus said, "Maybe not. But it is better to live wise than to die foolish."

*   *   *   *

On her way to the thane's hall on the tree-crowned low mount of Athelney Riada stopped at the low reed-thatched dwelling of Justus's widowed mother. Since Justus had been taken she was alone, and unsupported except for the little she could go on making from the plaiting of osier baskets, corn tubs and the reed mattings she made for those of the marsh- folk who could afford to buy or barter for them rather than make them for themselves. When the work was there she did field work on the yardlands for various carls whose acres bordered the marsh. Life was hard for her always, and harder now that she had lost Justus. But there was that spirit of doughtiness in her which had also passed to her son. No grumble escaped her lips. Bright-eyed, she had much of the look of a well-set hen, clucking and fussing, and ever busy.

Riada gave her a hare from her father and oat cakes

from her mother, saying, "'Tis no charity. A gift, Mother Alfrida."

"No need to explain, girl. But think not that I would be angered by charity. There is a time to be proud and a time to thank the good Lord for the kindness of folk. But for the nonce I make my way, and come the winter truly then I shall go to my son at the mineworkings. My only true need at the moment is one which can never be served."

"You have heard that I go for marriage with Arnulf the mason."

"Aye, I have heard. Quick 'tis—but then quick served you must be if what I hear is right."

"There is no certainty on it that I can tell at the moment."

Alfrida laughed. "Did you ever know Justus to make a bad job of anything he did? You will carry. And if he knew he would give you his blessing on your common-sense." She paused and then slowly her face-lines deepened with the sorrow of her thoughts and, after a moment or two, she said, "Why do you think they took him instead of butchering him on the beach? For a slave?"

"Would they take a man for slave and also his boat? Besides —they need no slaves to watch at sea."

"Then what?"

"Only God in His wisdom could know. He is gone—but although I go to be married to another I shall pray that one day he will return. Too late for me . . . but that is small sacrifice against his good."

"Arnulf is a good man."

"Aye, good. And good, too, will I be as his wife. But there will always be the seed pearl of longing in me for Justus. This I cannot escape, and good Arnulf needs no words from me to tell him so."

At the thane's hall Riada found his lady, sitting at the un-shuttered and unglazed window of her room which overlooked her small garden, busy at her needlework. At seventeen when she had been married she had been slim, dark-haired and beautiful. She was forty now with five living and four buried children to her name. Fat now but well settled with it, she was a woman of great common-sense and little patience with those who looked backwards instead of forwards and were always complaining of Time's losses and disappointments. She set Riada to carding wool while she worked away at a new altar cloth for the priests' chapel, and as though Riada had already been with her some time and they had long been talking, rattled on, "So you have lost Justus and will take Arnulf? Well, my lass, when you are my age you will know that there are good men and bad men. And then—which God keep you from—those who are good sometimes and bad sometimes. And those are the worst to deal with for you never know when you are going to be wrong-footed. Know, though, that I grieve with you for Justus for he is or was—we must leave that never to know now—one born to do great things. Many a time he has sat there and made me laugh with his sauciness, and the next minute have me sitting open-mouthed that he should have such an old head on young shoulders and should have such dreams . . . aye, strange dreams. Did he never tell you them?"

"No, lady."

"Then neither will I for sometimes they frightened me and sometimes otherwise. Let that be still, though. Suffice, Arnulf is a good man. One peg drives out another. When you are young that is the law. So now—do you think you will carry?"

"Only time can tell me that, my lady."

"'Tis no rule with women. I have always known. Nine times. And profited by it for on rising I have said as much and my man has always wagered against it and lost. With my last I won from him a silver mirror, the handle worked into the figure of Venus—which cost him dear to have made at a Winchester smith's workshop to my own design. One day I will show you. You think it odd that a Christian woman should choose a pagan goddess?"

"Is it not, my lady?"

"Idiot. She was worshipped before Christ came to earth to be crucified for our sins. She served her turn—for that she should be remembered in our present wisdom. This argument I have had with the priest and he—somewhat grudgingly— agrees with me. Ah, yes—and when you go back remember to tell your father that my lord, the Thane of Athelney, returns soon with the men of his fyrd. For this year the fighting—what there was of it, little, praise be the Saints—is over." She paused for a while, and then said gently, "You think I am hard and speak too lightly of your loss? That I take Justus's going with no heart?"

"No, my lady."

"Which, of course, you say from courtesy while you think otherwise. But know, that in these bad days it is wiser to hold one's feelings close. But know also that my heart grieves for you, and his poor mother. In a little while the priest will be here and we shall go to the chapel and you will make your confession to him and be absolved—though he may impose some not too tiring penance for you—and then we shall pray for Justus's safety and the hope that one day he may return. Unlikely, as you have common-sense enough to know. God alone knows. Keep faith. We will pray for his return even though it will be too late for your full happiness."

"My lady, I would pray for that with all my heart and all my soul."

"There, there." The thane's lady petted Riada's cheek gently. "You are a good girl. Before you go I will give you a length of Frankish cloth to make a wedding mantle for yourself. Mind you, I would it were something better. But the Franks are a poor lot at weaving . . . Now, wipe your eyes and look cheerfully. God is wise and His hands ever sure.'"

*   *   *   *

The *Fafnir* was ghosting on a light westerly wind, the up-Channel tide under it, almost at its full. A thin autumn mist lay over the sea. Now and again, its veils lifted so that Oric standing in the bows could catch a sight of the not distant coastline. At daybreak they had left the cliffs of the Isle of Wight far off on their port bow and were now much closer to the land. The ship's water casks were running low and the crew needed provisioning.

Oric went aft along the board walk between the oarsmen

who sat with their long sweeps half-shipped and idle, each man knowing full well what lay ahead. Joining Noth Oric said, "You remember this place ... three years since?"

"Aye, the little village at the foot of the forest."

"With a sweet water spring and cattle pens. And now the fruit picked from their apple garth to store against winter. My gut groans at the thought of the taste of sharp pippin. Take her in and let them see us—and so let us see what they can muster. You read my mind?"

"Readily. Let them see us so that they make their muster and then sail past them as though we judge the nut too hard too crack."

"Aye, and as they sit to their meal before sunset we come back on the new tide. Half the men ashore and the rest at their oars."

Oric went forward and Noth put the steer-oar over to bring the *Fafnir* towards the shore. The great sail lost the little wind that lived and the resting oars were run out to the full through the oar ports and, at a call from the oar-chanter, began to rise and fall.

Justus, lying bound at Noth's feet since they had come near to land, watched the shore come closer and then, as they were seen heading towards the settlement, saw the place spring to life. Men mustered as horns blew ... and few enough of them there were. Women and children, carrying hastily snatched possessions, and driving sheep and goats before them, hurried for the security of the forest beyond the settlement strand.

Noth said to Justus, "Your countrymen are brave but not so often wise. See, a band of them muster to meet us, but when we come close and then turn away they will in their simplicity think we have been voyaging too long to have much heart for a fight. Such men think too readily that which their soul wishes for. And when we are gone, turned away by their warrior stance, they will call their kin back and broach the mead and ale skins and so—when we return—will be easy game."

Justus said nothing. His heart was sick at the thought of his own land so near and he lying like a trussed pig, helpless. The

Fafnir moved slowly under the oars a little over a bowshot from the shore and the waiting Saxon men followed along the beach, shouting and raising swords and leather shields. Then, as Noth eased the bows seawards, their cries turned to ones of derision and insult as they realized that the Danes had no heart for a fight. Noth put the steering oar hard over and the nose of the *Fafnir* swung seaward to clear the distant point of the long bay.

Noth put out a foot and nudged Justus, saying, "Now, tell me what they will do?"

"Why should I tell you something you already know?"

"Aye, why? We go, they think, to other and easier pickings farther east where men are less ready or fewer. What care they of them? Nothing—and so they go back to their huts and will take to the mead and boasting. And within a few hours they will have created a battle victory for themselves, telling how they stood waist deep in the sea and reddened it with our blood until we turned away with no longer any stomach for fighting. The story will live—a lie come to life as a truth. And, in truth, that is the stuff of much of men's history—tales told by braggarts."

Justus said with sudden anger, "You took me as I slept alone on a beach. Had I been awake with twenty marshmen you would have learned, had you lived, that there is another kind of truth which writes history—even though the ending of the story might have been all our deaths."

Noth laughed. "I know what you can do with your crafting hands. I begin to learn, too, the kind of fire which you have in your guts—so, heed this, it is a fire which you would do well to keep damped down until time has tempered your spirit."

The *Fafnir* went eastwards through the light sea haze and then, long after it had rounded the headland of the settlement beach, Noth took her out to sea to make a leisurely turn that would bring them back hidden far offshore of the settlement.

That evening an hour before sunset they went in through the haze which lifted when they were within two bowshots of the shore, and for the first time Justus saw Oric dominate his crew. Four men at the oars held the *Fafnir* offshore clear of

33

the first wave breakers. Oric led the way with his men, all of them disdaining their shields, all sword and scramaseax armed. They went up the beach with a great shout to play the game of Thor to find the settlement men unready and many of them drunk from the celebration of the ever-growing victory which coloured their tipsy minds.

Some men stood and fought, instinct strong and their brains clear enough to aid their hands and arms. Many died, going groggily to death and hardly comprehending it. Women and children screamed and ran, but many were trapped and given no mercy. And while half the raiding band stripped huts of autumn stored provender and the drying fish and meat which hung from the smoking racks, others filled the *Fafnir*'s water skins—and no man stepped aside until the ship was provisioned. But that done—then Oric pulled a burning brand from a hut front fire and tossed it to the tinder dry thatch of a roof. As the roof flared, and then another and another, the Danes, drunk with slaughter lust, stronger than any of the mead which would come later, put the hamlet to waste with burning brand and sword so that a grey smoke column began to climb the evening sky and drift eastwards down the coast. All this time Noth and his oarsmen held the *Fafnir* free of the wave break and Oric with four men, a wineskin between them, stood at the water's edge and kept watch on the forest fringe. And well this was, too, for as the ravens, kites and eagles began to drift seaward over the forest, drawn by the towering pillar of smoke, a party of armed horsemen came out of the forest fringe a mile to the west and put their beasts to the gallop along the strand. Oric shouted a warning to his crew about the huts and Noth at the helm of the *Fafnir* gave an order to his rowmen so that they began to ease the ship closer to the shore, holding her in shoulder high water, her keel, no matter the skill of the oarsmen, now and again grating the bottom.

Not yet drunk enough or slaughter-lifted into unwariness the pillaging party at the huts turned and ran for the sea. As they came one of them stumbled a little in the rear from the weight of a young maiden slung over his shoulder. The girl was dropped into Justus's skiff which had been used for ferrying supplies aboard and three Danes pushed it out through the surf. By the time the party of horsemen reached the settlement all the Danes were aboard, the great sail filling with the steady breeze and all sweeps working. That night, as the *Fafnir* lost the west wind to a mild northerly and heeled over on the first leg of a long tack seaward up channel, the young girl was stripped of her linen shift and raped by all those of the crew with a mind to it and then with cruel charity had her belly ripped open and was tossed overboard.

That night, too, a fire began to burn in Justus, a hate-fire for these men and all their kind, a hate-fire which through the days and months and years he would learn to contain but never lose, nor want to lose since from it, he sensed, could only come strength for the will which grew in him one day to meet such as these men, armed with sword and wrath. When Noth came on steering watch he turned his face from him.

That night, too—all this in the year of Our Lord eight hundred and sixty-six—a young man of much the same age as Justus, a fair-haired unsleeping youth of royal birth, lay alone in a small guest chamber off the great hall of a Wessex alderman near Hampton where he stayed now with his brother. Gone for the time was the habitual unease of his body, the mark even in one so young of early indiscretion, since he knew a greater unease at the thought of the ravishment that the heathen boatmen were spreading all through the eastern parts of the land and in his own Wessex. He was of the great House of Cerdic and his brother was Ethelred, become king this year. His name was Alfred. That day he had been one of the hunting party which had arrived too late to help the people of the shore village which the *Fafnir* crew had ravaged.

2

JUST OVER A week later with September ending, on a morning when a first rime frost was touching the flags and reeds on its banks, the *Fafnir* ran into its home river and with the tide under its bottom moved upstream to the small settlement of Gerskat which was Oric's domain. Gerskat lay in the far south of the Danish kingdom where the Jutland peninsula narrowed and ran to meet the borders of Old Saxony. Across the peninsular on its eastern shores lay the town of Hedeby, a good three days' ride to come at. The river was tidal no further than Oric's settlement where there was a small wharf, secure moorings, and an easy bank slope up which the *Fafnir* could be handled on rollers for overhaul and refit close to the open reed-thatched yard where Noth worked. On either side of the river the land was flat, marsh and lake covered, full of good cattle grazing, its waters rich with fish and eels, and its ground ways harbouring ample game.

Freed now from all bonds, Justus sat in the stern of the *Fafnir* and with a slow bitterness growing in him was a silent spectator to the welcome the Danes were receiving from their own folk—men who now seemed miraculously to have shed all their savagery, moving husband to take a wife's embrace, sweetheart to clasp sweetheart, while children danced and shouted around them. Some women there were, though, who stood silently eyeing the *Fafnir* to find the expected face of a loved one ... only to turn away after a time to nurse their grief before knowing the true tale of deaths which had bereft them.

And these were men, thought Justus, who harrowed any land that lay open to them, raped and re-raped women and girls until they were no more than bruised, and bloodied, almost shapeless flesh to be flung overboard or left to rot and make carrion food on far distant fields and strands. Suddenly here, even with so short a while to watch them, he could see that they had become men again and untouched by Woden's madness.

Noth came to the quayside and looked down at him without speech for a while, his face touched with sympathy and understanding. In the last three days when they had turned the long foot of his own country and run into the north and south flowing tides and a wind that carried the first touch of winter's coming they had drawn a little closer in understanding. One night when all but the watch rested and Justus had sat free at his feet in the stern, Noth had said out of nothingness, "You think men do evil from the love of it?"

"It would seem some do."

"No, we are all born with it. Each man lives within the egg of his life. Neither your saints nor our gods have ever been free of that. Evil comes from want—not greed."

Remembering that now, Justus began dimly to see the truth in the words. Looking up at Noth he felt a swift surge of gratitude towards the man but for whom he would have been butchered on the sands.

Noth laughed and said, "Your face has gentled. Now I speak like father to son. Come ashore. But before you touch this land put aside all you have seen—as the *Fafnir* men will put aside all they have done. There are no right words yet to wreak the shape of the twisted truth of men. Come now— guard your tongue and be patient. This is your new life, and I am your new father. If you think the Fates have dealt you hard—think of your Christ who took suffering to his bleeding bosom gladly as a man embraces his father. Come up, I say. None will touch you for they know you walk in my shadow."

And so Justus went ashore for the first time in his life to a new land. Until now he had never left the marshlands to move farther than Athelney or Glastonbury. As he followed Noth he made a silent prayer to God, asking only that one day his eyes would see those places again, yet knowing full well that God gives nothing to man which is not already waiting to be gained by his own incorruptible faith.

A huddle of huts ringed the mild slope of the slight rise in the land. On its eminence stood Oric's hall, reed-thatched the length of its long roof-run. Servants' and women's quarters made a short wing at one end and near to that was an enclosed cattle byre. The land sloping away to the east of the mound was broken into crop plots ... wheat and barley waiting for near harvest telling Justus even in his detached state that grain ripened later here than in his own country. Beyond this, where the river narrowed above tide-reach, its freshwater course snaked away into the flat wastes of the marshes and wild land. At the foot of the rise where it met the river stood Noth's boat shed. Its sides were open except on the north and east. On its river side a pine-trunked runway sloped to the water up which the *Fafnir* could be hauled to cover for winter overhaul.

They went through a leather-curtained flap in the eastern wall and across a small yard to Noth's lodge. Before they reached the hide doorway its flap was pushed aside and a young woman came running out. She flung herself into Noth's arms and they embraced and kissed and there was more laughter and kisses between them than words before Noth held her away from him and, nodding at Justus, said, "Gerda, I bring with me my new workman. He is of the Saxon race but steps ashore here no slave. He will sleep in the sail loft of the boat shed. I must now go to Oric's hall for the beginning of the telling—which will be long and not all happiness for some. Put a cauldron on for his washing and feed him."

Gerda laughed and said, "The cauldron heats now and food there is a-plenty cooking for I saw the *Fafnir*'s sail when it was no bigger than a flying swan coming in from the sea."

Noth turned to Justus and said, "This is my granddaughter, Gerda. She is a good creature so long as I beat her once a week. When you have eaten stay here with her until I come— which may be long—for I would not have you walking free and a stranger to most on the day of homecoming for all do not know yet that you are bound to me, no son yet son-like.

Now, into her care you go, and, if she treats you unruly, thump her as you would thump any sister who lacked obedience to a brother."

So was the beginning of Justus's days at Gerskat, days that were to lengthen into months and years, days in which at first he suffered from many blacknesses of mind, days in which loss bit into him without warning, touched off by the cry of a wintering curlew in the marshes, the same cry an echo of his own land, days in which acceptance of his position came slowly though he kept his feelings mostly to himself. But, when he could not, he would cross the footbridge above the settlement and walk away his blackness of mind and find with its going an added strength to his determination one day to find his way back to his own country and arriving there take at once to the fighting service of his king and so to live or die—as God willed—in the fight against the heathens who coveted his homeland.

That night he slept uneasily, disturbed by the absence of the *Fafnir*'s movement under him and by (though it would be some days before the great welcoming feast would be held in Oric's hall) the passing shouts and drunken cries of Gerskat men abroad under the stars, drunk with mead and the raw pleasure of being once more at home with whole hides and the warmth of wives and sweethearts to come. As he lay there he thought, too, of Noth's granddaughter who had boiled a cauldron of river water for his washing, found him a change of clothes, linen tunic and long woollen trews. Completely at ease with him, which surprised him, as though he were more a returned brother than a Saxon stranger, laughing sometimes, as they sought to fit some word or phrase of their languages into common shape, he had drawn comfort in her company after the brutality and hardships of his *Fafnir* days. He had liked, too, the way she had small-honoured him as her grand-father had ordered, serving him with good wheat cake instead of barley bread to sop up his stew juice, filling his cup with mead and then, to clear and clean his palate, bringing out a dish of the season's apples, small and green but with a taste of honey in them. Through all this—at first he had thought

39

from a shyness or embarrassment she might hold, but soon he sensed differently—she had plied him with questions about himself and his country. At home he would have found a first met young woman acting so to be forward and to be watched. But soon he had sensed that with her there was nothing but willingness to follow what was her own open nature.

Before leaving him to go down the sail loft ladder she had stood silently for a moment and then had said, "Justus—for now I get used to your name—tell me, did you have some sweetheart girl who now weeps for you?"

"Why do you ask?"

"Because if so I will make a sacrifice to Freya to bring her comfort. Not a big one for I am not full woman yet. But I will eat no meat for a week."

"Freya—that is your goddess of love I learned from Noth."

"Yes. I will drink no mead for seven days."

Justus said, "There is one. But I would want no sacrifice from you. I have already made prayer to my own God."

"And rightly so. I will do the same to Freya. Sometimes the gods need one another's help."

Despite himself Justus had smiled and said, "Do what you will. And I thank you."

Now he lay in the darkness, hearing sometimes the call of a night-wandering curlew from the flat lands beyond the river, and more often the noise of men shouting and singing, and the high pitched laughter of women and girls as they came away from the ending of the telling at Oric's hall. Sleep came to him at last and he never knew that Noth, on his way back from Oric's hall, climbed the loft ladder and looked in on him, and then let the silent wish run through his mind that the gods would keep this one with him, despite the lack of kin, to take the part of his dead son who had had the same crafting in his hands as this youth.

When he returned to his hut he found Gerda sitting on a stool by the red fire embers, waiting for him. He smiled, and said, "There was no need, little one, to wait. I need no help in finding my bed. Tonight the mead had no fire to warm me."

Gerda said, "Why did you bring him?"

40

"Because one day I hope he will stand in what would have been your father's place in my yard. He would be to most a simple Saxon marshman, not worth a place on a rowing bench to bring home as a slave. But he is more than that. Tomorrow I will show you a small skiff he built himself, fashioned out of his own mind, without help—except for the nudges which the gods too seldom spare for men. I brought it back—because we had lost our own landing skiff—and he with it. You understand his talk?"

Gerda laughed. "Mostly. But often there are words that float like ghosts of words of our own."

"The trick will come—from your side and his. He learns quick. He is god-gifted. Be good to him, as I shall be, and his home-sickness will go the faster. But be warned—until our people have used themselves to seeing a slave who is no slave, who is as one of my own hearth and heart— hold yourself with kindness, stay back from all but cheerfulness and courtesy with him."

"You chide me so soon?"

"No. I remind you that you are a woman."

"You look too far ahead, grandfather."

"Of a certainty. That is the way all men and women should look. Would I put to sea when a distant cloud tells me that there are thunder-heads and storm to follow? Or tread firm looking mere ice until I have tested it?"

The next morning the *Fafnir* men came down to the river side, many of them nursing sore heads, but all in good and far different spirits from any Justus had seen in them before. Here they were family men and young warriors suddenly passed from their long dream of voyaging, plundering and killing, to become again husbands and sweethearts, tender with their kin and long-sighing and heart-anxious with their girls.

As they hauled the *Fafnir* up the long ramp and handled it finally broadside on under the thatched cover of Noth's boat shed Oricson turned to Justus who had had place behind him and said, "Well now, marshman. Welcome to Gerskat—and let all that has so recently passed be forgotten."

"I welcome that, and will hold it for all the time I am here."

41

"You think the day will come when you will see your land again?"

"That is in God's hands. But one day I know it will happen. Just as one day you know that you will go to join the Great Army."

Oricson said quietly, "You will do me a kindness to talk not about that openly. Though I have not forgotten the death promise should we ever meet free and you find the courage to mouth me insult to my people. But let that be—for now the past is set aside. You are Noth's charge—and I do nothing against his law. So let us smile and be as friends—until the gods throw the dice for a change."

"So shall it be."

"Good. And to seal it I say that when you are on free day or rest from Noth's work, we will go together to hunt and fish and I will show you this land which is not unlike your own marshlands."

So began Justus's first full day in Gerskat. The *Fafnir*, mast shipped, lay under cover on its blocks, barnacle and weed growths mottling its bottom boards. Close by Justus's skiff had been off-loaded. With the ship-docking chore done the rest of the men went off and Justus sat on a trestle and waited as Noth first walked around the *Fafnir* and then came to the small boat. He stood regarding it for some time and then turned to Justus and said, "Truly, without help, all that came from your own mind?"

"Yes."

"You had seen nothing like it before?"

"No."

Noth walked away and from a bench he picked up a piece of wood and an iron tool. He came back to Justus, squatted on his hunkers, and tossed to him the piece of wood, saying, "Look at it carefully. It is as it was cut from its tree. What do you see in it?"

Justus turned it over in his hands. It was a small section of the slim trunk of a beech tree, still barked, from whose side projected a handspan portion of a side branch which had grown from it.

42

Justus smiled. "You mean what do I see in it which would serve your craft?"

"Our craft—yes."

Justus walked beyond the *Fafnir* to where a small ship's boat —probably, he guessed—of the same style as the one which the *Fafnir* crew had lost and so taken his as replacement.

He said, "Split fairly in half lengthways you would have two pieces like this." He dropped the piece of wood and held out his hands, his finger pressed closely together but the thumbs projecting stiffly but bent at the knuckles. "Shape them well and you would have a couple of tholes or oar pivots such as there are on this ship's boat. I would like to have thought of such a use myself instead of the sealskin loops I used."

Noth laughed, a rich, almost childish sound of delight. "The gods have gifted you. My joy salutes them."

"It was not hard to see."

"Not for you. But for most impossible. And how would you split a length of good straight-grained pine or beech or oak to make the clinker planking for a *Fafnir*'s hull?"

"Had I the tools I would cut it from the centre in wedges as you cut a good wheatcake, and cut it so for the whole of the length I needed. But one would have to have the tools to do so."

"All you would need is a hafted metal wedge with a good heavy hammer to drive it home—and such you will find in my tool locker, and many more besides, and in a month you will be handling them as though you had known them all your life."

"You say good things to me."

"I say truth. Spear and sword and battle-axe all true men can handle as easily as they breathe. But when it comes to the craft of ship-building their hands are as clumsy as pigs' trotters. Thank your God for your gift as I thank Thor for mine. We shall work together to build great war-craft. Aye, even to Hedeby we might be called in time to come to work on a king's craft that will make the *Fafnir* no more than a clumsy cygnet following in the wake of a royal swan."

Justus smiled. "No swan lived yet without first being cygnet."

"Your tongue works smoothly, too. Guard that it never runs away with you in the wrong place with the wrong man. Already it is becoming known that insult hangs promised but yet unspoken between you and Oricson. Be wise—let it lie like a sleeping dog."

"So I shall. So I must until the place and time is right for its speaking."

"You look forward to that moment."

"No, I do not. But it must come ... I feel the truth of it in me."

"Young blood. Forget it. Now, to that which has more virtue in it than any feuding or raiding or blood letting. I will make known to you the other tools of our craft."

Noth rose and went to his bench and from a box lifted out one by one, each wrapped against his sea-going in soft, greased kid leather, his ship-wrighting tools—augers for hole-boring, trimming axes, razor-sharp handknives for carving treenails and decorations, chisels for working grooves the length of a hull planking to hold its caulking, splitting wedges and hammers and tongs for forging and shaping nails and roves. And so began Justus's new life as an apprentice to a ship-builder, and also his first day in a humane captivity that was not to be without pleasure but never such as would soften the hard lust in him one day to find his feet on his own native soil again.

* * * *

A few days before the end of September Riada and Arnulf were married before the priest at Athelney. There was a small feast with their kin and friends and they slept that night in Arnulf's hut which lay on the northern slopes of the isle. Lying together under their rough blankets and a large deer hide coverlet, both of them naked, the sounds fading of their friends and family singing and laughing as they made their way home after seeing them bedded, Arnulf reached out gently and drew Riada into his arms. She came obediently

44

and joined the warmth of her body to his and they both lay so in innocent embrace for a long time as outside the owls and the nightjars called.

After a while Arnulf said gently, "I must speak to you now of the thing which is between us and of the joy which moves in my heart and flesh."

Riada said, "There is no need for words this night. I am wife and you are my man. You have shown me kindness and love. There is nothing I would deny you."

"No. There are some things which, for our happiness and ease of mind, must be denied. You may begin to carry another's child—and if you do it will be cherished by me as though it were my own. But life is hard enough without me wishing to add other burdens to the ones which the good Lord has seen fit to place on us." He gave a little laugh. "Though it is hardly meet for me to say it, but you will know the innocence it holds, we will from this day be as brother and sister but a little more since my manhood is too strong to hold back from warming you in my arms at night."

"You speak gently. And I read your thoughts and will word them for you to save you more. You would not that we move into full closeness until I can tell you that I do or do not carry Justus's child?"

" 'Tis so, and must be so with you, too. Every child has a right to know its father. And every father and every mother the right to know the truth of their seeding together. So, we stay as we are now and take the part pleasure only, contenting ourselves with the less until we can freely move to an adoration of each other's flesh with truth unshadowed."

"Is it not too much to expect that you can hold to that? I would not, if it were, make any bar."

"It will be hard. But it will be done—yet a few small alms I ask. That I shall not be denied the joys which I know now. Small alms I ask—small alms I will hold to."

"You are a good man. But you are a man—and I need no oath swearing on this. I will do and be always as you bid. And I thank and praise you for all you have said—and you shall have such comforts from me as you wish."

45

"Then we say no more of this."

He held her more closely to him, his mouth taking hers and his hands moved over her breasts and thighs until the joy in him rose to his throat in a low moan of ecstasy so that out of loving charity she took his manhood in her hands and gave him relief.

The next morning they packed their small belongings and Arnulf's tool pannier which was bulky for as well as stonemason he could work, too, in wood. Both of them well-laden, they took to the marsh paths and began the long day's journey which would take them to Glastonbury, where a good month's work waited for Arnulf on repairs to the small chapel there and where they were to lodge in one of the priest's huts on the lakeside at the foot of the high tor. The work was to prove longer in its doing than Arnulf had expected and on a morning two months later as Riada rose and stirred the fire embers to life, feeding it into flames with dried rush and hazel twigs, she looked up at Arnulf and smiled as he finished cross-banding his working trews and shook out his mason's surcoat to pull it over his head.

She said smiling, for affection and respect for this man were deep in her now, "Work well and be happy today."

"Is it not so with me every day?"

"Today more than any other it must be. And full man and wife we shall be when we bed this night. By God's truth and woman's knowledge—I tell you now that I carry Justus's child."

For a moment or two he said nothing. Then he went to her and laid the back of his large, work-worn hands against her cheek and the wet shine in his eyes proved him near to tears which rose from joy. He said, "I will be true father to the child—before God I swear this. And—" he grinned shyly, "— if it is God's will—it shall not lack for brother or sister to command and bully as the first born."

To his surprise Riada suddenly put her hands over her face and began to cry. Anxiously he raised her to her feet and, putting his arms around her, said, "What ails you?"

She looked up into his face and, smiling through her tears,

46

said, "No ailing. I weep for your goodness to me. God in His wisdom took Justus from me with one hand and with the other beckoned you with your gentleness and love." She suddenly wrapped her arms around him and buried her face in the cloth of his rough linen working shift.

*　　*　　*　　*

The year thinned towards its end, and long before the mid-winter pagan feast Justus had formed a truce with his restless, determined spirit. Hope was easy to keep alive but waiting with the itch for freedom and a return to his own land was hard at first. Without loss of spirit or determination he came to terms with it gradually. Three balms of some power he had—his work with Noth, his acceptance by the settlement folk, and his lopsided friendship with Oricson. On land he found the Danes were people more or less like his own except for their religion—and amongst them he sensed after a while that there were more than a few who looked towards Christ worship with a curiosity that, for all their wariness, alerted their minds as a bright feather or polished stone drew a magpie.

Greatest comfort, apart from his prayers and hopes, was his work with Noth. The long ship shed over which he had his sleeping quarters now held the *Fafnir* up on blocks and undergoing a refit. Alongside her, blocks had been set and the keel scarfe of a new raiding craft laid. Men with time on their hands, or wish to evade their huts and women and children, came and went, sitting and talking, telling tales and now and again mock correcting Noth at his work and always, when more labour was needed, were ready to help carry trunk lengths and timbers from the great open weathering stack at the back of the shed.

Working with Noth Justus learned fast for there was in his hands the same gift as in Noth's though not yet so sure. He made many mistakes with cleaving axe and hammer, and it was a full month before the use of the shipwrighting tools began to act sweetly under his bidding. His hands grew new calluses and he delighted—almost forgetting his own state—when at last he had the art of making the planing adze shape out a true curve to floor timbers—though when Noth put him to carving a miniature dragon's head for a ship's prow he made a sorry job of it. Gerda on seeing it giggled helplessly and said it looked like a pig's head. Noth grinned, too, and said, "Give him time. When you first set to pluck a goose you finished up looking like one yourself."

More apt he was with Oricson out on the marshes and flatlands where—their feud put to sleep for the time and an odd comradeship growing between them—he had no disadvantage with anyone. They netted the still pools between them for the fat carp, built duck hides and floated decoys to bring the wintering birds down, and could each man fit and flight three arrows from their bows to make their kill before the birds rose in panic and Oricson put his water dog to the retrieve.

On one such afternoon after they had made their kills and sat under a mist-pale late afternoon sun, Oricson said, "My father . . . in hall last night—you heard?"

Justus said, "I have no place in the hall—unless bidden. Noth has asked for it for me but not even he could turn your father. As for me, I do not quarrel with that."

"Ah, yes . . . well, it comes from my father's wisdom. There are still our people here who in drink might bait you. And you miss little once the sagas and songs are done and drink takes hold, and even those you can hear freely by standing outside—which you have done I'm told. But you have not heard from Noth the news?"

"No."

"Next season the *Fafnir* stays in the river."

"Why?"

"Because the king is to be at Hedeby and my father is called there to the gathering."

"So the *Fafnir* stays in the river. But not you?"

"No. I shall go north a little and find another dragon ship."

"Against your father's wish?"

"You read the runes right. Against his wish—but I go."

"And stay—maybe to help your people against the East Saxons?"

"For one who is forbidden the hall you have long ears. But it is no true secret. Already it begins."

"Why do you tell me this?"

"Because I need your help when the time comes. My father is set on taking me to Hedeby with him when Spring breaks."

"And why should I help you?"

Oricson laughed and said, "Pity 'tis that you were not born a Dane and we could do things together in comradeship. But you will help me. Three times I have dreamt the same dream. A dream of our meeting. It is in my memory as clear as a painted rune stone I once saw of Sigurd's slaying of the dragon and then again of his roasting the beast's heart to eat—and you would laugh if I told you the name of the dragon."

"There is no need. I know it already."

"You cannot."

"I can. It was *Fafnir*. And look not surprised. When I sup with Noth and Gerda she would have from him each evening some story of history."

"Well then, you know. But do you promise help?"

"I do—since it is to bring us together in my own land, and, a free man with a sword in my hand—though your dream did not write the end. What would you have of me?"

"That when the time comes you will row me out at night to one of the small islands up coast, not far. You can go out on the tide and back with it for easy work. I cannot go over land with all my gear and weapons and war tack. No one will think to name you. No hard task. We go out on the top of the tide and you come back on its turn. The tide season will be picked for that."

"So soon you come to me, a slave, for help?"

"I would take help from a pig if it had boat and could row."

"You could steal my boat and loose it free in the tide."

"Ah, no. Since I am doomed to kill you, I can deny you no foregoing courtesy."

For the first time since he had been in this land Justus lay back on the ground and laughed, freely and loudly.

49

When he finally sat up Oricson said, "Now come—give me your answer."

"Answer I will give you. If you believe in your dream you already have it."

"Well spoken. And now, in return, I say here that if any in this place ill treat or ill speak you—except my father, of course—I will take your part. Oh, Saxon boat-builder, how you have lightened my heart. The day I kill you I shall truly grieve. But now—since you are man and have a man's needs—I will do you a gift act. There is a widow, not young but comely still, who lives nearby. She will at my bidding give you the ease of body that young blood needs."

"You speak with good intent, and I thank you—but I would rather take the dogs and hope to turn up a winter hare. And take no offence at my words."

"As you say, but on the way back I will show you where she lives."

That night Justus lay in the sail loft long from sleep. Oricson would be away and had worked a manner of doing it. That, too, must he do. But for the moment he had no shadow of a thought as to how he could make it come about. One day, though, he knew it would come to him in answer to his nightly prayer for a light to be given him to show him the way.

*　　*　　*　　*

Late one afternoon, when Justus was sitting on the edge of the rough sleeping shelf he had built for himself in the loft of the boat shed, Gerda came up to him to fetch him to eat in Noth's house. She stood before him, dark hair bound with a head cloth, her face rosy and shining with the cold, and looked down at him with a small smile touching her lips—a smile that was only absent when she scolded her grandfather or she was working at her loom, concentrating as she moved the shuttle skilfully along its course, building up her patterns and colour blends. Then, nodding towards a slim length of willow switch he held in his hands while he worked with one of Noth's carving knives, she said, "What is it that you work at that makes you frown and purse your lips, Justus? So often I find you here before supper doing this."

He looked up and grinned at her. He liked her for she was kind to him always, and from her singing about Noth's hut he had picked up from her snatches of songs and lullabies which were gentle and tender and made a change from the sea and war songs that Gerskat men sang when the drink ran through them.

"This?" He held up the willow rod.

"Yes. Is it some Saxon magic? A way of making a spell? If so would you work one which made me a handsbreath taller and three notches of my belt buckle smaller about my waist?"

He laughed. "You are as you are. So be content for I tell you what you are is good for the eyes. A full sheaf of barley stands on its own."

"Maybe—but it is not all men who think so. Now tell me what is it you make there?"

"I count the days of my life since coming here." He nodded to the shelf above his couch where lay three or four rods similar to the one in his hand. "A notch for each day and then a longer one for special days." He reached up for one of the rods and held it for her to see, "Look—the first long notch was for the day I arrived for that was a special day."

"But unhappy?"

He shrugged his shoulders. "I do not notch my feelings— only the passing of time. And this long notch, the next down, that was for All Saints Day when November coming in began to thicken the lake ice. And on another there are the day notches and the long notches for the day of the birth of the Holy Babe and so on."

"And the long notch you have just cut on the rod in your hand?"

"That is for Candlemas. The day of the Purification."

"Which means?"

"Some time I will explain it all to you if you wish to know."

"Why should I not? Gerskat women stay here while their men go off—and when they come back what do they tell us of the world so far away? The young ones talk of battle and

51

blood letting and angry seas—and paint it bolder than in truth it ever was, I fancy—and the older ones say little for fear of a slip of the tongue which should shame them before their kind."

"And good Noth?"

"Ah ... he wearies me to sleep many a night with his fantasies. Great ships which will hold two hundred men, and he draws maps on the sanded floor of lands and seas and traces the keel marks of the *Fafnir* for me, and sometimes to tease he tells me of islands where all the men are two-headed and double-wedded so that they speak the truth to one wife with one head and with the other give the second wife the fables and lies he would have had for the truth. And he says he has seen many a mermaiden suckling her twin babes as she lies on her back riding the smooth thrust of the sea's swell. What would you tell, had you a wife?"

"I should have to know what kind of wife it were first. Some wish truth, and some guess it—and others run from it. Which would you choose?"

She laughed. "You do not trick me so easily. How should I know? But I find it good that you mark the days." She paused for a moment and her face turned solemn. Then she said, "To no man of Gerskat could I speak these words. I am not ill-favoured I know, but then neither am I of a form and face that the bards would sing. One day some man will ask for me—but only, I know, when his patience runs out from asking others first."

"Then such men although they see are blind."

A small smile lightened her face and she said gently, "Now I tell you something which you will keep to yourself. Sometimes Freya touches me and a curtain rolls back. 'Tis dream-like but no dream since it can happen as I pour swill for the pigs or grind barley to flour. So was I touched a few days after you were brought here."

"And this touching—what was it?"

"Of you. You sat by the mere side. It was high summer, the reed warblers were hard flighting to feed their young, water rails moved over the lily pads, and the fishing ospreys sailed high against the sun—and there you sat with a ..." she giggled, "... a face as long as an overpacked mule. And then as you watched the waters you saw something in or on them which I could not see—and you sprang up and you thumped the top of your head with your fists and shouted for joy, and your face was aflame with happiness. Now is that not strange?"

"In truth, yes."

"And more—to me, and I say this perhaps overboldly, it marks that the gods have linked us for some purpose."

Justus stood up, smiling, put out the flat of his right hand and gently touched her cheek, and said, "There is no denial in me. There are many things not to be understood in this life until God throws light on them. Now let me guess what we eat for supper—and I need no help from anyone for I saw you plucking a brace of wild duck this forenoon. And no doubt good Noth sits turning the spit already and wondering where we are and will perhaps nod off and let them burn. Come."

He took her arm and led her to the loft steps. It was the first time he had ever touched or held her so and the feeling of woman under his hand woke a disturbance in his body which he had not known since the far off day when he had lain on the dune sands with Riada.

As they sat on their stools around the eating bench later Noth said to Justus, "Gerda has been scolding me that I let you sleep in the boatshed loft now the cold weather is so well set—though the gods know I have slept rougher and longer in cold as a young man without harm."

Justus said, "I have made no complaint."

"Aye, which makes it a little worse—since your silence reproaches me. So, I have settled it in my own mind that until Spring comes you should bring your bedsack here and sleep on the floor with the fire embers for warmth. I was wrong to treat you slave fashion. But then—" he grinned, "for your own sake I thought it better to treat you so until our Gerskat people had used themselves to you. Too much kindness too soon would have marked you for disfavour. But now you sleep here. I know this also is the wish of Gerda who has begun to scold me so boldly that many another man would have given her the back of his hand."

"Do that ever, grandfather—" Gerda grinned at him, "and I will pack my bed roll and trudge to Hedeby and find service in the house of some rich merchant. Aye, and turn wicked and take liberties with his Frankish wines and kick up my heels and make warm heifer eyes at the young men of the court."

Sternly Noth said, "Such talk puts your backside at the risk of my hazel staff."

"I but tease, grandfather. But now I will talk like the woman of the house. What have we here but this one room with our sleeping shelves, a space off for my loom, and one small side lodge to hold our salted meat and fish and stores? You are Noth and known through this country for your craft. Now I risk your hazel staff. Justus was a prize you brought back, and half made him son because you saw in him and his work that which my father had. I shame you for your ways."

For a moment or two Justus saw the anger flush across Noth's face, and then slowly it faded and the shipwright rolled his eyes in mock amazement and grinned, saying, "Ho! ho! Now the she-cat turns and spits. What should I do with her, Justus?"

"You could without loss hear her out, Master Noth—and beat her if her words prove unpleasing. And what her words will be will be as new to you as to me."

"Gently spoken. Take no sides between blood kin." Noth turned to Gerda, and went on, "Speak, wild cat."

"Your name is known in this land. Four years ago you made the King's craft. Chief Oric takes pride that you stay with him. When he drinks in other's halls he boasts you to swell his own pride in you. Now, I say, do what you planned before my father died. Build two more rooms on to this lodge. One for all our stores and your hunting gear and your fishing nets and spears and in it a bed for Justus."

"And the other room?"

"There would I have a high bed-shelf, and my loom, and there when the men come to talk and drink with you would

54

I retire gladly since I have heard all their tales long ago except those which would shame me but that without me could be spoken freely. You are Noth of the Dreams—" she turned to Justus and went on, "Aye, they call him that when, in mead, he talks of dragons that will fly with men on their backs and of kindly whales that gently swallow men and then let them see from their whale eyes the under ocean world and ... and ... and ..."

Noth laughed. "See now—she pulls up like a blown filly. But there, my Gerda, I am not such a fool or mocker to stamp you down." He turned to Justus. "Did you sit in my place—what would you say?"

"I would be coward and give her what she wants for the sake of peace, rather than eat undercooked flesh and heavily salted oat porridge for days on end. But this I say, too—I am content with what I have."

Noth was silent for a while and then said, "Well, I am not. You speak gently. And I return it. All shall be as Gerda asks ..." he grinned, "... more properly—demands. We will settle to the affair tomorrow. But since I give Gerda what she wants—then before you go back to the loft we shall drink a little mead and she shall sing for us ..."

Later, lying in the darkness of the boat loft, it was some time before Justus found sleep. When he did it was to drift off with the memory of Gerda's good voice singing.

> Skefil bound by
> Freya oath
> False lay with
> the far land queen
> Frost bright her jewels
> Pearls are the tears
> I weep
> For lost brothers
> to wreak
> Red sword revenge ...

*　　*　　*　　*

Coming down from his sleeping loft the next morning Justus found Oricson sitting on the end of the plank stack.

Oricson said, "You sleep late. Was it the mead or Gerda's singing that wearied you? Look not surprised—I passed late from my own affairs." He winked. "Since you are set to do me a favour—I will do you one. Nought to do with Gerda or her singing which is fair, but always of lost loves and broken hearts. A battle song you will never hear from her—and with some rightness for they are for the men to sing."

"And the favour?"

"If you will call it such—for it brings no comfort to you."

"Your generosity is left-handed."

"Maybe. But I thought you would wish to hear the news from Hedeby which my father brings. No secret soon for it will be sung throughout this country—and bring suffering to yours."

"And so the secret which is no secret?"

"This country is small and poor and yet the people grow more every day. A hogskin will hold only so much water. My father says that soon there will be no years wasted in summer coast raiding. Though, mind you, that does not run for this year. You know well that too many years ago to count, your people, the Saxons, took the country from the British. Your people were as we are now." He laughed. "That makes us some kind of kin. Now soon comes our turn. Already—and this I did not know—it has begun. Many of our fighting men who would have come back for the winter have stayed in your land—in the country of the East Saxons. So it begins—and with the Spring and with your help I go to join them. No longer is plunder the whole world. Men are hungry for land and conquest."

"Then you need not my help for surely your father will willingly let you go?"

"No. My father is cautious. He will wait a whole season to see how this new move shapes. And I must stay with him—though I shall not. Those who go first claim the rich prizes ... land, women and slaves ... and, should a man prove himself beyond all others as a warrior, then a kingdom is there to be carved from your Saxon lands for himself."

Justus said coldly. "You must first catch your game before you can roast and eat it."

"Aye—and it is that first part which makes my blood run hot. But then comes the land—what have we here? Wilderness and marsh and such good land as there is is already too little to feed all our mouths. War dreams fire the mind, but it is land hunger which truly presses a people into battle. So, Saxon Justus—I tell you all this—and for reason. You are still set to help me go?"

Justus smiled. "Why should I not? Since I cannot here give you the insult you crave to loose your sword—then willingly I help. And one day I shall follow you and pray that somewhere we shall meet."

Oricson shook his head. "I would wish it—but I doubt it. There is no way for your return. Gentle yourself to your Fate. Aye ... let my people take you as one of them in time and perhaps marry plump Gerda. With wife and kinder, comfort at night, and Noth's protection you are well set. Nobody will give you passage to your own land. Aye—you should take Gerda. She is ready for it—since it is three summers since the man she would have taken is dead. He went out on the raven's wind with his comrades and none returned. Gerda grieved, but I think Noth grieved more for the loss of their craft for it held place for many more men than the *Fafnir* and was the apple of his eye."

That day when Noth came into the boat yard they picked out the timber and planks which they would need for building the extension to Noth's dwelling hut and, as they sat at mid-day with the oat bread, cheese and thin cider which Gerda brought over for them, Noth said, "You grow friendly with Oricson despite your sword promise?"

"Aye, I do."

"Why?"

Justus shrugged his shoulders. "He is the shadow shape of myself—no matter the feud between us."

"If he should coax you into some venture to escape his

57

father and it were known, you would live no longer than a few breaths after your confession—which would come unwillingly from you by torture. Be wise—deny him whatever rashness he presses you to. He is no kin of yours to claim help from you."

"Kin we are—not by shared blood but by shared sword oath."

"You will not be gentled or led by me?"

"I would were it not for a thing which works within me, that tells me that to help him is to help myself. But do not ask me for the answer to that riddle—it has yet to be shown me."

"A word from me to Oric—truth or no truth—would settle the matter."

"If you must speak it you must."

"You know I will not. I know, too, that nothing will ease the itch in you to return to your land. Is it for the girl of the sand dunes?"

"That in part—though I should be ready to find her married and with children, and if such were God's will, then such it must be."

"You would attempt a crossing in your little skiff?"

Justus laughed. "Would you?"

"If there were no other way—and I had the fire in my belly which you carry. But—"

"Aye, *but*—there lies the turning away word. Even so, if God is with a man there is nothing which is impossible. If I were about to try it in the right season—what would you do?"

Noth smiled. "It would depend on the mood of my mind when the time came. But—since the seasons of good sense never change, I would say you went to disaster. I have seen many a fair summer's day with the sea as flat and bright as polished emerald turn within an hour into an anger which would swallow you. Now, no more talk. Let us get to work on Gerda's demand. After that there is much to be done, here in the yard and at the Great Hall for this summer Oric holds a feast for a royal party which comes from Hedeby."

58

So, through the new months of the year 867, the notched sticks above Justus's bed in the addition to Noth's hut growing in number, the work went on with the overhaul of the *Fafnir* and the slow rising into shape of the new war craft, and Justus found with the passing of the days a form of content and peace which made truce with his slow burning longing to go some day back to his own land. In that time things took their course. Some of them such that, to begin with, Justus found himself trapped by them, and some of them from which—despite his desire—he had no wish or will to fight off.

He picked up swiftly the main skills of Noth's craft—and in this work found a wonderful ease, a peace which came from the crafting of wood and the joy in seeing the rising of the curved strakes of the new dragon ship and the keen pleasure of a chisel in his hand as he cut out the long caulking grooves in the hull planks.

One night at the end of a day when the eye began to look for the return of the cuckoo and the swallow and the tadpoles in the meres wriggled to free themselves from their spawn jelly, and a night when there was feasting in Oric's hall for the visit of his brother and party from Ribe, far north along the coast, as Justus lay on his bed boards, the firelight from the main room flickering through the chinks in the partition wall at his side, Gerda pulled back the hide curtain of his doorway and looped its folds on the holding cord. The fire glow shadowed and part lit the room as she came in and stood above him. Over her shoulders and round her body was wrapped a coloured blanket of her own weaving.

She came to his bedside and looked down at him, smiling, and he looked up at her in silence, his face plain, deep shadowed by the firelight. She said calmly, "Tonight—though he means not it to be—my grandfather will sleep drunk at the Hall with the other men. Though, should he come back he is too wise to take any shock from what he might see. In his mind I think he has long foreseen it."

Justus said, "You speak calmly."

"And you. And that is how it should and must be

between us—and also kept between us. I would come into your bed, not for love, but for a comfort long denied both of us. There can be no offence to anyone in it. But if you should turn me away—for honour of Noth—then I shall leave with a different kind of happiness than the one I come for. Do we need more words?"

"You speak gently and offer comfort. But that taken and given could seed its growth in you. I would not wrong you or Noth so."

She shook her head. "My true love is dead. What could not happen with him will not happen with you. I seek the comfort all men and women need, not husband or child." She grinned suddenly, "Perhaps though, Saxon, you find me ungainly and not to your liking?"

Justus laughed. "You misread me. We should do no wrong to any others. And as for liking—is it only by the eyes' pleasure that it has to be proved?"

"For some. But gladly I see not for you." As she spoke she dropped a shoulder and slipped the coloured blanket from her body and then lay down beside him. He took her in his arms and held the warm, fulness of her large naked body to him. Then after a while they moved, without hurry, through growing caresses, to their full giving and taking, and when it was done she lay in his arms and with his cheek against her he felt the wetness of her slow tears and, because the same thing was in him for another, he knew that she was thinking of a long dead lover while even in his mind the shadow of Riada stood afar off. And so the same thing happened again and again with them when the times were right, and whether Noth guessed the truth between them or not, he said nothing.

*　　*　　*　　*

A month later while Arnulf still worked at Glastonbury, stone-walling the old decrepit wooden nave of the chapel so that it should become properly one with the stone built chancel, Riada was brought to bed over early with a child and was helped with the birth by the wife of one of the workmen who served with Arnulf. It was a boy.

Arnulf going to her when all was done, stood looking down at mother and son, smiling. He bent and kissed Riada's cheek and then with the tip of a work callused finger he gently touched the child's warm, flushed cheek and said, "While I have worked today I have prayed for you and the child. Bad work—for my mind was not with it. But for that I will make amends. Tomorrow it shall be done again and on one of the high wall stones I will cold chisel that this day was a boy child born to the wife of Arnulf the mason who gives praise to God." He grinned. "But on a stone so high placed that no monk nor abbot will see it. And so what is the child to be called?"

"Since it is a boy—that is for you to name, my kind Arnulf."

"No. We hold to no custom. And I am no man to know how Justus's mind would have worked. You must choose the name."

Riada reached out and took one of his hands, fingering it fondly, and said, "Since you ask it of me, I will. I would have him named Otta."

"Why so?"

Riada smiled. "Because it sounds like otter—and although Justus hunted and killed them it was never with any true joy for he loved them and their ways as they moved through the waters. He said to me once that if he were free to choose another life after death he would become otter because they live so freely in the world of waters closed to all mankind— yet can come ashore and with one shake be of this world. His mind was full of such thoughts."

"Then Otta he shall be. And today is a day of double happiness. My work here is near finished, but the good abbot tells me that King Ethelred calls to him to supply one mason for work that has to be done on the abbey at Wimborne and he is sending me since in standing I am the best such workman he has. So soon you will see a king's court and the royal athelings and the fine ladies who wear velvet and silk and touch their cheeks with red ochre for beauty and have hands so finely and softly skinned that their finger tips slide across the rare silks from the lands of the Inland Sea as a rounded pebble moves across unflawed ice."

"I am content with that. But also I am content wherever you are. And this I say, too—there is no greater happiness I look forward to than to bear for you brother or sister to follow Otta. And it must be said, too, for your comfort, that the mourning for the loss of Justus dies away. That is God's comfort for all great losses ... time and each day's passing brings in a healing acceptance of God's wisdom which is beyond our true understanding."

But when Arnulf had left her Riada looked into the red, creased face of her babe and with sudden hunger in her sought there to see the shadow and shape of something of Justus's face which lived undimmed in her memory. Then she laughed suddenly and said aloud, "Oh, sweet babe ... what is there to see, but a red-boiled, wrinkled, long-stored russet apple of nothingness? But be teased not so soon, my love ... you are of his flesh and will be of his boldness and skills." Then from laughter she was moved to weep for the father lost and the goodness of the husband newcome.

*　　*　　*　　*

On a day when Justus had cut a long notch on his willow stick to mark the coming of Pentecost and the bean fields beyond the great hall were full of opening flower blooms, he sat on the mere side late one afternoon between the finishing of his work and the hour for eating at Noth's hut, baiting up a long night line to set for eels. The sky held light still, the sun just past setting. Late Spring was over the land and bringing with it memories of similar days in his own marshlands. Natterjack toads called along the lake's edge, a hatch of alder flies hung above him and sometimes flew into his face. A few heath moths were early abroad and, away to his right, he could hear the splashing of carp and barbel as they swirled in excitement feeding in the shallow waters. The odour of the white flowers of the garlic plants he had

62

trampled to come to the water moved strongly through his nostrils. Out on the mere he watched a swan rise on her island nest of dead reeds and turn the eggs beneath her, and a hen harrier came drifting across the new weed growths waiting for the movement of unwary coot or moorhen. All this he had seen and known back in his marshlands. So he had sat many times readying a night line and, sensing her more than hearing her, had turned to see Riada coming towards him. True love memory stayed clear ... this Gerda had said to him one night, her eyes wet with tears, after they had made love. Noth now knew about them but had said nothing either out of wisdom or from compassion more for Gerda than himself. Perhaps also, too, in the hope that he would truly join himself with her. The people of the settlement would accept that now. He was no longer stranger, no longer Saxon in their minds. He was Noth's right-hand. Maybe, he thought now, there would be wisdom in accepting his lot.

At this moment he heard someone coming to the mere edge from behind him. He turned to see Oricson who gave him a wide grin and sat down beside him. They sat in silence for a while and then Oricson said, "This is the season when Frey moves the blood of men and Freya puts longing in the loins of women and the beasts and birds and other creatures join the mating dance. This is the time when you should ask Noth for the hand of Gerda and so gain full liberties here for my father would then give you hall pass as other men. You think I say that mockingly?"

"No. But not with understanding. I am as you. It is beyond the sea flights all my longing."

"Then I am free to burden you. Five nights from now I would go out on the tide at last light and have you take me to my meeting."

"The weather could be wrong—unless you have bribed one of your gods."

"If so we wait until it is right. As I shall be waited for on one of the coast islands since I have sworn to the dragon leader that he shall have a third of all my gains from the first year. He will wait."

63

"And your father—what story will be poured into his cup?"

"No story—for I shall leave none. But I shall take all my war gear that day and drop it in the mere. Sad and bitter loss, but wise for you—since none would believe that you could take me so burdened in your skiff, which is true. My new war-leader will have all I want waiting for me—and dear it has cost me. You drop down river at sunset and I will meet you at the mouth. You come back on the tide and troll a little for a few fish. You are freeman and have night-fished before at the river mouth. You think I would go and have you suffer . . . aye, maybe butchered? No, that would be to deny the gods—we have a score to settle and in your own land. The gods have set that. And by the gods it will happen Saxon marshman for it is clear in my mind now that they have fingered you. No, come back innocently and late from your night fishing and warm yourself against Gerda's fat breasts—"

Justus turned swiftly and his knife just touched the skin of Oricson's throat. "If you wish to die and feed the eels in this mere foul not that name to me again."

For a moment or two Oricson stared hard and bitter-faced at Justus, his lips and cheeks muscles working tautly. Then slowly he relaxed and laughed gently, saying, "Oh, that you were my brother and we could go together. So, now, gently, I give you word that I say nothing more against the good lady. Nought would I do to make the gods turn mind and so never give us free meeting—though by those same gods I see not how it can ever be future truth—yet do I believe it." He stood up. "It is settled?"

Justus looked up at him and after a moment shrugged his shoulders, saying, "I am bound as you are to the will of your gods to the pattern set for me by my own. I take you because meeting again there must be." Justus smiled suddenly, and went on, "Do you not see that it is my whole belief for from it springs not hope but certainty that one day in my own land I shall kill you."

"So truly do I believe otherwise—but by my gods. And

64

when you are dead I shall sing a skald of it which will make our names live forever."

"Give me no more of your dreams—but make yourself of service and help me with this fish baiting."

3

As Justus stood at the bottom of the slipway by the water's edge, the tide now half-way to full, shipping aboard the baited lobster pots which he meant to drop at the river's mouth, Noth came down and stood watching him in silence. Swallows flew low over the river, dipping their breasts to it from time to time.

Noth said, "You would I come with you and drop the pots?"

Justus shook his head and smiled mischievously, saying, "It would serve you badly. For with the weather set so fine I have decided that I shall go west and begin the long row home and that would give you no pleasure."

Noth laughed. "I take you for wiser man than that. Your craft is sound enough—but you know the saying? Flesh wearies long before wood parts. If the gods oathed you a sea all mill pond for twenty days then you might have hope and even then the gods for reasons no man can read often turn as fickle as young girls touched by Spring fever in the blood. Go lay your pots." He raised a foot and pushed the boat free into the river and stood watching as Justus took the oars, now set no longer in leather loops but in rowlocks shaped like the *Fafnir*'s and fitted by himself.

Returning to Gerda in his hut Noth found her sitting on a stool, the stone quern before her as she ground at the corn for milling with her pestle. For a while he sat silently watching her, and then said, "The next time Justus and I are timbering in the forest we will cut for you a trunk length to fashion you a wooden quern."

"Why so—this has served you and your father before you?"

"Aye, but it comes to me now that all our family's teeth

have suffered from such service. As you grind the corn the grit from the sides of the quern gets mixed with the flour and then—"

"And then—" Gerda laughed, "—long before old age the bread which gives us life has worn down our teeth. For years you have said so—but no wooden quern has arrived. Why now do you make the promise to fashion one?"

"Because there is something astir in me which demands some offering to guard against a thing I fear."

"Speak your fear—though I may guess it."

"Justus."

"There is no surprise in me. You love him as son. And he gives you honour. But you do not command his heart's longings."

"Aye—that is truth. And what of your heart's longing?"

"It remains, wrapped now in easeful sorrow. He will never be husband to me. I am content, and know from your goodness that you take no shame in me."

"That is true. So tell me—why do you not, unlike other women, keep a blinded singing bird in a wicker cage to make music for you?"

"Should I take joy from any creature's cruel loss?"

"Truly said. I take joy from the skill of Justus's hands in the yard, delight in the growing magic that begins to show in his craft work. And think me not wrongly—I fear for him. That he will do some rashness. He has gone now to lay lobster pots— the weather is fair set it seems. But behind the face of the skies and the smoothness of the sea there is always the shadow of change. He longs for his land as a caged song bird longs for freedom—and the longing could over-flood his common-sense. Were he not to return from his lobster pot laying it would give me no surprise, and then no surprise to learn one day that his skiff had washed ashore north or south of here. It was made for lakes and meres not the changing waters of the sea to become, maybe, the idle sport of the world serpent Midgardsorm."

"In part you misread Justus. Risk he will take, but never court foolishness."

67

"I pray that to be true and take comfort from it."

With the sun lowering over the western rim of the sea, Justus laid his pots in the river mouth and then rowing farther out felt the lift of the north running tide under the skiff and turned her bows with it. He ran along the coast for a while with the tide under him and then came ashore on the dune coast at the place which Oricson had named. Oricson came from between the dunes to meet him, smiling, his face flushed and his eyes wild bright with his inner dreams of the future.

He said, "You keep your word. There will come no harm to you. My father thinks this day I have ridden east to make court to the family of the one he has marked for my bride—a willow wand of a girl with dark, sea-anemone eyes with whom I would gladly bed—but not wed. She will weep no tears for my loss since she did but follow her father's not her heart's longing. Now—give me the oars. I will take us up coast and so spare you for the tide-run back. When you put me on the island you will see no one. Which is just—since under torture you can give no shape or name to the one who helps me."

Justus smiled. "You would spare a tear, though, for me should it ever happen and come to your knowledge?"

"Aye—but from one eye only."

"Aye, if that be, save the other eye for me. I will do you the favour of closing it in death when our day comes."

"By Odin, I could wish you were coming with me and things were different. Why should the gods have sent me a near-brother and placed the death oath between us? Still—" he grinned, "—I will take the path marked and wait eagerly for its crossing with yours. By the gods, this skiff moves well with the tide-run under her ..."

Oricson took them up the coast until the lip of the westering sun was nearing the far horizon line and then went seaward under the last of the tide to one of a group of low, sand-duned islands which lay close off shore. He ran the skiff aground, jumped out and held her bows while Justus took up the oars.

"So we part—but before we do, Saxon, let us put the insult talley even between us. I asked you once if your marsh girls were web-footed and with scales on their backsides. Now—" he pushed the skiff free on to the water and as it drifted away, went on, "—give me back your insult words, that I may brood on them."

Justus smiled and shook his head. "I have given you help—so be content with that. You shall have my words one day—and they will be the last you ever hear for, having spoken, sword or spear or axe will send you from this world."

"So be it." Oricson raised his right hand in farewell and turning headed for the dunes of the island. Justus pulled away from the beach and out into the sea run between the island and the mainland to meet the slack of the tide turn which would take him back to Gerskat.

But the tide turn soon proved little help. With it came a change of wind to the south, a wind that rose quickly, fighting the tide and raising a strong and confused sea against which the low freeboard of his craft offered scant safety. By the time the first stars began to show against the dusking sky the bottom of the skiff was awash beyond help of his wooden baling scoop and he was forced to turn her bows towards land. When he reached it after hard labouring with his oars, he jumped free into the surf and, taking the painter, dragged the skiff up part free on the sands and then lifted her bows to free water from her enough to get her well ashore. He rested for a while to gain strength and breath, and then dragged her into the dunes well above the high water mark where he sat filled with anger and frustration— not from any fear he had had for his safety for he could have abandoned her and swum safely to land, but from the loss of a wild hope which, even knowing its foolishness, he had cherished that one day he might take her and attempt the long crossing to his own land under oars. Gone was that hope.

He took the long walk over the dunes and the marsh tracks to the Gerskat river bridge above tide reach, and walking brought him calm and fresh resolution. He had nourished an impossible dream ... now he had to clear his head of all vain thoughts. Oricson had gone. One day he would follow him and to make that a truth he had to find some way of turning his dream into hard shape. He needed a bigger, more sea-worthy craft, one that he could manage single-handed under oars against calms and by sail when the wind offered even the most miserly help, and in some way he had to do it openly for there could be no way of keeping such crafting secret in Gerskat.

When he reached Noth's house Gerda and her grandfather were sitting by the dying fire embers waiting for him.

Noth said, "Gerda would have had me call a party and go search the shore for you. But I did not think it would be your wish."

"The need was not there. After laying the pots I rowed a little along the dunes with the last of the tide for the evening was fair. But with the turn of the tide the wind rose suddenly against me and the skiff could not master it. So I came ashore and pulled her up the beach and then walked back through the dunes and marshes. If I have caused you some fears, I ask your forgiveness."

"You have it. Gerda has kept hot wheat biscuit and boiled eggs for you. So eat."

Gerda setting his food before him said, "I had fears for you."

"For that I am sorry." Justus smiled. "Did you think I had turned the skiff's nose westwards?"

Noth laughed. "The thought may have been with you—but with you dreams take second rank to common-sense."

"Aye, the trick is to join the two somehow."

Gerda said with a set face, "I do not like this talk. We both know what is in your mind—a wild dream. Now, I go to my bed."

When she had gone Noth said gently, "And do I know what is in your mind?"

"I think you do. But you are against it."

"I grow old and find fewer things in life to rouse deep feelings in my heart. Yet with age I find I can read the

70

feelings of others shadowed in their faces more easily. Do you think it will come to pass?"

"Not without help."

"Why so?"

"Because I need a craft, bigger and sounder than the skiff."

"You have its shape already in mind?"

"No. But that will come."

Noth laughed. "You would do better to hide away on one of the coast trading craft and try to make your way south to Frisia and beyond and then hope for a merchant crossing to your own land."

"All that? And maybe two years in the making and no certainty that I might not on the way be taken again for slave? No." Justus smiled, enjoying their talk and its frankness. "When I go it must be by sea."

"And, of course, you would have me help you?"

"No—for that might bring you harm."

"Yet by yourself alone it cannot be wrought. Perhaps I could be tempted."

"How?"

"That I know not. But for every man in this world there is some gift or happiness to be found which will bring him against his will into the trap of charity and good will. I say this with no joy, but only because I know that there are some falcons which can never be manned to come back to the falconer's fist." He frowned suddenly, and went on almost angrily, "Now speak no more of this. Get to your bed shelf and nurse your dreams."

* * * *

That summer, in the year of Our Lord 867, two days after Justus had cut his long notch to mark Lammas, Oric came into the boat yard where Justus and Noth worked together and sat on one of the trestle benches. Justus carried on with his work as Noth went and sat by his lord, but his ears were pricked for all that Oric said for he had been absent at Hedeby for a month and from Hedeby all news came.

71

And news Oric brought. As soon as the year's weather had set fair for campaigning, the army of the Danes – which had over-wintered in Thanet, and was later joined by the Spring dragon men who had made an early raven's wind crossing – had passed into the land of the East Saxons and had gone north in great force to the city of York. Here at first they were resisted by the Northumbrians under their king, Ella, but in a second attack they took the city with great slaughter and plunder and Ella was slain and the Northumbrians made peace with the Danes and bowed to their possession of the city and the lands of Northumbria. For the time being the eyes of the Danish were turned away from the lands of the West Saxons. But the listening Justus, who had now long come to have a wider knowledge of these people and their battle and land hunger, knew that this was the beginning of a very different period of danger for his people. Fewer and fewer dragon craft would put out in single or small company to pillage and plunder during the season of fair winds. He had now that which had never been in his mind when he had been taken from his own marshlands ... an understanding and growing wisdom and foresight that made him mark the rising yeast of the future. These heathen Danes and their like near neighbours farther north in Norway and Sweden were no longer battle-geared pirates lusting for plunder. Land hunger was biting deep into them. And the rich prizes of permanent conquest lay no more than a week's sailing from their shores. The thought of Oricson crossed his mind and his cheek muscles tightened in anger.

At this moment Oric called to him, and he went over to where the two men sat, enjoying the sun, each cradling a burrwood cup of mead in their hands.

Oric looked him up and down in silence for a while and then said heavily, "You carry deceit within you."

"I do, my lord?"

"Aye...for it has come to my ears how this thing was managed against my will. Speak me the truth for upon it your life's thread wavers now like that of a blown spider's

72

seeking a fair wind to take it to first anchorage on some bush or reed clump."

For a moment Justus's mind darkened and he knew the clamp about his guts of growing despair. Then, as he raised his head with some proudness to reply, he caught Noth's eyes and read in them—though he knew not how—the counsel the old man would have given aloud were they alone together. So, he said, "Seek from me what you wish, my lord. Truth will be my answer."

"Aye, and truth may be your death. You helped my son to leave this place, to go against my orders. Did you not?"

"I did my lord."

"I ask not how—for that I know in part and the rest can guess. But give me the why. There could be no true friendship bond between you."

"There is only one bond between us, my lord—and that stronger than friendship. We are sworn—for insult given and insult yet to be given when we next meet—to a death oath to be settled when I come to my own land again. He asked my help and I gave it for there is perhaps more virtue in a death than a friendship oath."

"Your pride sparks like a spitting pine log. Now, were you in my place and I in yours—what would you do?"

Justus was silent for a while, and then said calmly. "I am near slave here, my lord. But within myself I am free man. Were the places changed and Oricson slave in my country would you have him forget or forgo his own true self? Your gods and my God have shaped us as brothers in a tie mightier than any of blood. We are bound as on a coin marked with our different designs on either side. One day the coin will be tossed—and the fates will decide which way it falls to earth."

"By Odin, you speak boldly."

"Would you have me lie to you? To cringe and plead like a slave? I am no slave—though gladly I do the work my master sets, and I hold myself with decency in your domain. I am set against Oricson and he against me. That tie is beyond brotherhood—and stronger."

73

Oric's face darkened and then suddenly cleared. He turned to Noth and said, "What do we do with this proud marshman? He talks boldly ... aye, and with some reason. Aye and more too—he calls our gods and his to stand behind him in his certain charge on the future." He laughed suddenly, "Counsel me, Noth. I am lost against such stripling beliefs."

Noth raised his work-grained old hands high and, with a shrug of his shoulders, said, "If the gods have marked them, then they must run. As for me—no better craftsman has ever laboured in this yard. As for Oricson, though I have no vision to see how it may ever come about, he would take it no favour to have father step between himself and the destiny the gods have marked for him. My lord, these days young colts have a different way of thinking and a new shape of pride. Let the wind blow—the gods direct it. But—" he grinned "—I should weep to lose such a craftsman."

Oric rose and then, after a little shrug of his shoulders, said to Justus, "Forget your dreams of destiny. Settle here, take a wife and sire children. Be content. Noth's place awaits you ... though I pray the gods not for many years yet. When that day comes you shall be given place in my hall and be true Gerskat man."

He turned and walked away. Justus, too, would have turned back to his work, but Noth stayed him, saying, "Wait. 'Tis now my say, and now my turn to school you. Oric has been just and understanding. So too will I be. First, because my craft is now yours and you know that your skiff could not outlive an hour's bad weather, it follows that you must have a boat that would. And since men tire in bad weather—it must be a craft that with sea anchor would outride storm while you rested in your sleeping sack on the floor boards ... aye, and need much else beside. I name not these needs. You must look into the future, see them and know what to fashion to meet them. Remember this—men tire, but the sea and the wind rest never. Fathom those wants and when you can meet them come to me and we will talk again. And do not forget the words I gave you on the night you proved your skiff could never take you back to your own country." He rose. "And now to work—and no more words on this matter until you can answer question with true answer. You were lucky to find Oric in good humour."

*   *   *   *

The young fair-haired man came up the river path towards Wimborne. The October sun touched to dull fire the first turning of the river trees and a few new fallen leaves drifted on the face of its current. Not far distant the grey bulk of the Abbey rose against the cloudless blue of the morning sky. A red riding cloak hung loosely from his shoulders and the front of his doeskin jacket was open over a loose silk shirt caught about his waist with a belt from which hung his short scabbarded sword. He rode, lost in his own thoughts, and was caught mildly unawares as his horse suddenly snorted and danced a little across the narrow path. His left hand tightened on the reins and schooled the beast to mannerliness as he saw the reason for the animal's mild alarm.

From the side of the river a young woman had risen clear of the fringing willow-herb and wild iris growths. Seeing him and recognizing him she blushed, then dropped her head in a low bow as she half curtseyed. On her back, shawl bound, she carried a small babe.

Seeing her confusion, he dropped his free hand from his sword grip where it had gone instinctively, and smiled at her. Being in good mood and always pleased to look upon a fair-faced woman, he said easily, "You rise from the reeds like some river goddess. What do you there?"

"I gather cress, my lord."

"You know me?"

"Who in all the Saxon lands does not, my Lord Alfred? Also I weave rush baskets and mats for your good mother, the Lady Judith."

With the smallest wry twist of his lips he said, "Step-mother. And your child? What fortunate father gives it name?"

For a moment or two Riada was still from searching an

answer. Then, since from his easy manner she took confidence, she said, "I am from the marshlands, my lord, where his true father lived and courted me until he was taken away as slave by the dragon ship men. Then good Arnulf, the mason, married me and gave the child his protection."

"Ah, Arnulf, yes. The mason. He works now on the abbey. He is a man of great goodness. And of great skills. And—" he smiled again, "—of good fortune to have captured a marsh and river goddess. And what name had the true father?"

"Justus, my lord."

"And the child?"

"Otta, my lord."

"Strange, but I like it." Then with a frank, open smile he reached down and took a handful of the cress from her basket and pushed it into his mouth and chewing on it said, "I thank you fair-haired river goddess. God be with you and your child."

He rode on and now, with his back to her, his face became set and hard and he fought with the rising of a familiar unwelcome pang of lust in him. This life, he thought, was full of battles which might one day come to an end, but where was an end to be found to the strife between good and evil which warred in every man's breast?

When Riada told Arnulf of her meeting with the king's brother, he laughed and said, "He is a wild one still but of a great goodness of heart. They say that there is talk of a marriage for him with a Mercian princess ... aye, that is if anything is left soon of Mercia and its people. The talk is that the Danes are there to stay. And, if stay they do, their appetites will grow and their eyes turn south towards Wessex." Then pausing, and the look on his honest, plain face familiar to Riada so that she knew what must follow, he said, "You are well?"

"Yes, Arnulf. I am well. But pull not such a long face. There is time enough and to spare and the good Lord will be kind and send brother or sister for Otta."

Arnulf grinned. "That is my prayer—but for a son with

76

good hands and a head for heights and a long life that will bring great churches with towers that reach to the sky. Sometimes, you know, I dream of such buildings ... with a great bell tower and with spires reaching to heaven as though they were fingers eager to touch and prove the blue stuff and weave of the sky."

She went to him then, put her arms around him and kissed him and, since he had not yet washed, felt on her lips the fine sharp touch of mortar and stone dust. Had Justus never existed to be still alive in her mind she knew that her love for Arnulf would have been as absolute as the love she had had for Justus.

*   *   *   *

So, summer slowly wore itself away and Justus accepted the challenging promise made to him by Noth—though he could not fathom the meaning or the conditions of all those matters which had to come to full conjunction first. He lived and worked content with the shadow of hope, and this was enough for him because he saw that behind all men's half-promises and veiled meanings lay his destiny. Understanding would come through his own vision and hard work.

Noth had scorned his skiff as a craft for any sea-crossing. And with truth. So he set himself to the shaping in his mind of a sea-boat which would, with all the safety a man could hope for under God's skies, take him back to his country. Time and again he felt that he had it in his mind and he would take charcoal stick and on a freshly planed board would draw his design for Noth, and Noth would sit and study it and the man's words of cavil would burn in his mind righteously but wounding. *How would you alone, in a sudden bad wind and sea, sitting in the stern at the steering oar get forward safely to lower the square main sail? And again— What will you drink when your water skin is empty—or would you overload the craft with a cargo of skins so that the first following sea poops you? Hunger a man can long fight, but thirst soon brings madness to the brain. Do you fancy that in your plight your*

77

God would give you the power of His Son to walk upon the waters?

On this last Justus said, "How know you that happened?"

Noth smiled. "You think there are none of your religion in this country? Some already lay it open. Others keep it close in their minds. Monks and friars have sturdy legs and a faith that fears not death for they know Paradise awaits them. You think none of our dragon men have not taken the eastern water ways to the Great Inland sea? Many have ... aye, and taken their daggers and carved their runes on the backsides of many a naked old Roman goddess in Venice and Ostia."

For a moment or two Justus made no answer for there came a sudden itch in his mind which stirred him to a fuller understanding of Noth's kindness and charity. He said gently, "Have you talked to such men ... such monks ... and perhaps borrowed some of their belief and charity?"

Noth laughed and said, "I have ears and eyes and a mind. I keep them open—for that is what the gods gave them to us for. But seek not to move away from your task. The riddle is clear, and waits an answer. A pair of oars will help you only in near coast waters. But for a crossing you must make only the wind serve you while it blows and all this must be managed as you sit at the steering rudder. And at the times when you must sleep then you must shorten sail and let the craft ride safely to the oncoming seas and wind. Another man aboard would rid you of these problems for you could sleep in turns. But you will be alone." He laughed suddenly. "Oh, Justus, your face is as long as a mule's."

Touched to some anger Justus said sharply, "Then I take comfort from that! What is more stubborn than a mule? There is an answer to every difficulty."

"Seek answers then. With their coming—so will come the shape of your craft. But I give you warning. Should you find the answers I may not give you leave to build the craft."

"Why not?"

"That I cannot tell you."

"There is little charity in the answer, my master."

"So be it. I am a man, not a god. Every loss needs some gain to heal the wound it leaves. Now ... no more of this talk."

That night long after Noth was asleep Gerda came to Justus's bed in the darkness. They lay together after their love-making and as she rested her head on his bare shoulder he felt the wetness of tears on her cheek.

He said quietly, "You weep. Why?"

She answered, sniffing gently, "Because you have given me back some part of lost happiness."

"Is not some better than none? I have learnt to be part content with loss—and that in most measure through your kindness. This which we have is a shared comfort."

"But a comfort to be broken for some while. I would have told you before but could not bring myself to speak the words until this night. I go tomorrow to Hedeby to do service in the King's household for his lady at the royal looms since my work has been seen and praised by her. It is a command and an honour and not to be gainsaid for that would give offence and dark mark my good grandfather."

"But you will return in time?"

"Aye."

"And who will serve good Noth with you gone?"

"The widow Fursila. Her man was lost on the *Fafnir*'s last sailing in a raid they made long before you were taken. She is a good woman and will come each morning and stay until you and Noth have eaten at night. So this is parting ..."

"But I shall still be here on your return. So dry your tears." He said it to comfort her, but in his heart he hoped it would be an untruth. The year was well over its full and with stubborn disregard of all the difficulties he had marked the season of the coming year's steady raven's wind of Spring as his time of going. Marked it, and forced himself to believe it, for without belief there was no tempering the longing for return which ate slowly at his heart. He took her into his arms and comforted her with the warmth of his body. But there was bitter anguish in him as memory, refusing all denial, returned of his lying with Riada on the warm dune

79

sands with the sound of wave-break and lark song making music for their shared ecstasy.

A week after Gerda had gone, his day's work done, and the evening still full light, he went into the marshes to set traps in the lake outlet streams which ran into the main river. The big eels were beginning to take their spawning run to the sea now. Whither they went no man knew, but run they did and were fat and full grown and good eating and the widow Fursila—though loyalty kept the framing of the words from his mouth to Noth—was a much better cook than Gerda, whose mind was never far from her loom and the bright patterns that came alive from her imagination.

His trap setting done, he sat by the edge of the lake, and began to think over the problems of his boat building. Some difficulties, small ones, he had already overcome. But there rested the main one which rose again and again in his mind each day, teasing him and sometimes making him bad-tempered.

Brooding over them now while his hands idly and to no purpose slivered the bark free from a withy branch, he stared moodily into the water. Long-legged water-skaters moved on the mere's surface skin and black and silver water-boatmen went round and round in a mad whirligigging, doing nothing it seemed and never tiring. Watching the water-skaters, he thought, why should not a ship be built, carried high on legs like theirs, each ending in a small float ... a small, enclosed, well-caulked float? He laughed to himself at the nonsense. Then, as he watched, a white-winged butterfly came down and rested on the water-skin with its closed wings raised. A gentle zephyr of wind, moving across the water, gently took the insect's closed, upright wings and for a moment or two before it took off the butterfly moved over the water like a fairy boat before rising into the freedom of the air.

Justus sat there, watching it move away over the iris and reed beds, and for no reason he could find in himself he felt a coldness at the back of his neck, an icy touch that moved through his body and somewhere in his mind memory stirred

... something ... someone's words. And then slowly they came to him with a growing lift of excitement. Gerda ... long ago ... but now her words came to him as though she were standing at his side. He sprang up suddenly and thumped the top of his head with his fists and gave a wild shout as her words rang clearly in his memory ... *And then as you watched the waters you saw something in or on them which I could not see ... and you sprang up and thumped the top of your head with your fists and shouted for joy, and your face was aflame with happiness ...*

The next morning Justus went about his work in a brooding mood, reacting absently to the talk and jokes which passed between Noth and the other two craftsmen who worked in the yard on the now growing hull of the new *Fafnir*. But late that afternoon when the other workers had gone Noth came to him where he sat on the edge of the boat slip, watching the tide run out.

Noth said, "You have been like a bird in moult all day. What ails you?"

Justus looked up at him and said, "No malady. The other side of that coin, perhaps. Yesterday I sat by the waterside and a butterfly landed on its stillness and raised its wings so—"

Using the stick he held in his hand he drew on the sand the outline of the butterfly's raised wings, and then went on, "So it stayed and then a gentle wind took it and it sailed across the water, wings still raised, like a boat sail. But no square sail that a man would have to go forward to raise and lower—a sail that a man sitting in the stern, if hoisting cables and runners were so arranged, could manage without leaving the steering oar, and a sail also that in bad weather could be shortened so that, with the steering oar lashed to a fixed position, a man could sleep while the craft held a true course with the run of the seas ... and ... and ... well, other things yet to come for which my mind now reaches ..."

Noth smiled and then after a long silence said gently, "Something of it I see in my mind ... though such a sail

81

and so rigged I have never seen." He stood up, and went on, "Tomorrow after work is done, put a clean white lime washing over the wall boards of the loft, and then with charcoal begin to draw your dream as you have seen me draw the shapes and curves and craft fittings of the new *Fafnir*." Then, his face growing solemn, he added, "You were sent for my joy and my sorrow. The gods have put their mark on us. But the gods always leave man the last freedom. This form of craft may come to life—but there will be no sailing to your homeland in her unless the return gift is given."

"I lose the meaning of your words."

"It recks little ... but there is kindness hidden in them for you if the gift is made. Now come to supper."

"Nay, I have no belly for food this evening. And, too, I ask your leave to quit my bed in your house and to sleep in the loft as I once did."

"Why so?"

"Because things might come to me in the night which I would want to mark on the lime-wash wall. I would have nothing escape me."

Noth shrugged his shoulders and sighed. "Better, perhaps for me," he said, "had I left you on your dune beach to sleep and wake and never know that the *Fafnir* had watered there."

"You riddle me."

"Then add that riddle to the others that now wait your answering." Noth spat into the sand at his feet and turned away.

So, while the weather held good, through later summer into autumn and until the first coming of the snows and the mere ice thickened, Justus slept in the loft and the virgin whiteness of the freshly limed wall slowly filled with shapes and sections of the details of the butterfly boat, some accepted by Noth and many, at first, condemned with a grunt of disdain and then later with a wordless nodding of his head approved at their re-limning. But when winter finally set and the children and youth of Gerskat took to the thick ice with their bone skates there came a day when Noth, the weak light of the winter afternoon fast fading, looked at the spread of drawings and said slowly, "There is much still that I would have better and some things that will find no answer until your craft takes the water. But there is always that in life. No man achieves perfection. The search for it outlives all generations—such is the law of man's striving. So, now, begin the search for the proper shaped tree lengths and branchings. What you do must be all your own work. I do no more than play the lute and mark the melody for you to follow."

That evening Noth ate in the Great Hall with Oric and his men. Drinking horns were filled but the company stayed sober. A lute player plucked his strings and sang to them as the light from the great fire and the wall sconces cast moving shadows over the dark underbelly of the long roof.

After a while Oric said to Noth, "Something shadows your mind. Shadows perhaps cast by some burden?"

Noth turned to him, surprised, and said, "Does it show so clearly?"

"Only to me—for the bond between us began the the first day, scarce able to stand or manage our limbs, that we fought and played here on the floor sand of the Hall. But from that grew the true friendship we know now. Would you say something to me which is meant only for my ears, and being said is locked within me for ever?"

"Aye, good Oric, my lord, I would."

"Then say it. It shall ever rest between us. 'Tis perhaps something that links your Gerda and the Saxon slave?"

"You read my troubles. I will be frank with you—and after the telling, if you gainsay a promise I have made, then that promise shall be broken. But remember in the hearing that I truly believe the gods were with me when I made the promise."

Oric laughed. "You have a face as long as a horse. Speak on."

"'Tis of Gerda and Justus. Until she left they shared bedboards. For that I find no shame. He is man and she woman and in him she found something of my son who took the raven's wind and never returned—and of another who also lay under the covers with her, but could never raise within her the fruiting of a child."

"So it runs sometimes."

"Aye, and so she—thinking the fault of seeding lay in her— went to Justus's bed without fear. But the gods willed otherwise. She has gone to Hedeby and begins to carry child by the Saxon."

" 'Tis no great matter, though the child—should it be man child—could never sit in this Hall unless I gave the word. Which for your comfort I say I would. So, the matter is settled."

"There is more. And never did I doubt you would speak less than with your present goodness. But this more may turn you to anger against me."

"You are as roundabout in reaching home as a boy who knows full well that a thrashing awaits him there. Know you not that there is nothing that I would deny you for the goodness that is in you and the friendship between us? Spit out this fig-seed that has stuck in your teeth so long."

So Noth spoke directly and freely about Justus's dream to build a boat for escape, about his butterfly boat dream, and of how he, Noth, would let him use it for the sea crossing if, unknown to Justus, the boon of a boy child were granted to Gerda, a child—if the gods were kind—who would have his father's craft to follow him when the gods called.

Oric heard him out, for a moment or two his face darkening, and then, the cloud shadow of anger passing, he said, "You took much on your shoulders. And ask much of me, a simple man, who believes that there is no good bargain where there is not gain on either side. From the asked kindness—what do I gain?"

"You lose nothing—be it man child or girl child. If girl child—Justus stays. If man child—Justus goes and with a fair semblance of it being an unexpected escape. And never will he know that he leaves me his son to take my craft.

Gerda returns not to Gerskat until long after the gods have had their way. But either way there is great honour waiting you—for this little craft he wishes to shape is but the shadow of greater ones which will be built here ... craft that can be used for war or trade. Wherever they are seen ... aye, long after your death, people will say—there are the keels of Oric of Gerskat whose mind the gods fired to a kindness which brought him greatness."

Oric for a moment said nothing. He lifted his drinking horn and drained it. Then, wiping the over-spill from his lips with the back of his hand, he suddenly laughed and said, "Noth—you have missed your true craft. When you die be happy for you will be called to give counsel in the Halls of the Gods. But I would not wish you to wait for death to be happy. Do that which you wish. But this, too, I say. Your Saxon man must know nothing ever of all this. Be it man child—he goes and Gerda returns. Be it woman child then Gerda never returns to Gerskat while the Saxon lives. And be this also—for I would have no bawdy, taunting skalds made around it to shame me—all this lies between us. And believe this, too. For no other man in the world would I have promised that which I now make gift of to you. Now let us fill our horns and drink and forget these new passed words."

*   *   *   *

In the depths of that winter Riada and Arnulf walked back after midnight Mass at the abbey on which Arnulf was still working. The stars were set diamond sharp in the sky. From the river meadow a bittern called eerily and a barn owl drifted like a wraith between the trees of the apple garth and moaned briefly at the lack of good hunting. In the small log-framed lodge which the monks had put at Arnulf's command the serving girl was already abed with the infant Otta lodged in a withy basket beside her. Arnulf took rush taper to the low fire and lit two of the wall sconces. He then set two pewter cups on the sturdy pine table he had fashioned himself and filled them with strong Frankish wine.

Sitting together, facing each other over the table, they smiled at one another, contentment for a while muting all need for words. They touched their cups together and drank a silent Yuletide toast. Then Arnulf reached into his belt wallet and brought from it a ring which, taking her hand, he slipped on to her finger. Looking down at it Riada caught her breath at its beauty. The ring was gold and set in a circle of gold filigree was a gay design, worked in cloisonné coloured enamels, of a bouquet of flowers. Its beauty caught her breath and, as Arnulf laughed at her delight, she leaned across the table and kissed him, saying, "It is too good, too beautiful for one such as me. Only an Atheling's lady could wear it with right claim. Oh ... Arnulf, good Arnulf, it must have cost you dear."

He laughed again at her delight and said, "You talk now with a housewife's tongue about cost. But you are no housewife. You are the marsh goddess ... slender as the willow, your beauty flashing bright as a winging kingfisher. And speak me not in woman fashion about costs. The good bishops and abbots pay me well. On what should I spend their gold more fittingly than on a heaven sent wife and tender mother of Otta? Take your present and wear it with pride."

Riada kissed the ring and then raising her face blew a kiss back to him.

He laughed and said, "Now drink. The abbey was cold. The Frank wine will fire your flesh."

Riada raised cup to him and they drank. Then looking at him in silence for a while, a smile soft lining her mouth, she said teasingly, "And now, since take deserves give, you wait a present from me?"

"To love and be loved and be with you is all present I need for it renews itself with each day's coming. So be happy on that score."

"And so it has been. But this mass-night it is not to run so for truly I have a present for you. You should know, Master Arnulf, that I am two moons gone since I have known the flow of Eve."

For a long while Arnulf remained seated, looking at her,

his mouth slack opened giving his face a flat stupidity. Then suddenly a great grin brought true line and life back to his face. Grinning he rose and shouted, "Praise be to God! Praise be to God!" Then suddenly concerned, he came to her, put his arm round her shoulders and said seriously, "You feel well? Nothing ails you? Ah, this late cold night air. You should have told me sooner and we would have not risked the coldness of the abbey walls."

Riada said nothing, but she hid her face against his doeskin surcoat and put her arms around his body, and he held her firmly until the shaking of her body eased and died. But, and she shamed herself for the undying weakness in her, there was, until she banished it, the memory of Justus's arms around her as they had lain on the warm sand and the air had been full of the cries of the fishing terns hovering over the returning tide run.

*   *   *   *

Some days later, in the first bitter cold days of the New Year of 868, the young Atheling Alfred rode at his brother's side back from boar hunting in the great forest of Selwood. Both were warmly cloaked and trewed, boar spears resting upright in their butt sockets, short swords hanging from the stout leather belts worn and buckled about the flap of their great cloaks. No man of importance or sense rode unarmed even in these days of rare calm since the Danes were far north of them many days ride beyond Mercia. Their hot breath plumed in the sharp air and their eyes marked the bridle pathway for frozen water patches.

King Ethelred, rake-thin against the sturdiness of his brother, young still, but his face pale and drawn above his neatly trimmed blond beard, coughed a little and spat his phlegm aside. There was the familiar Cerdingas strain of looks between the last of the sons of King Ethelwulf.

He said, "I would have you first to know that with the first Spring thaws, I go north to Mercia."

Alfred smiled. "I know your news to come—it has passed

to and fro in the women's bowers for some time. As rumour foreshadowing truth."

"You pass too much time in women's bowers, my brother. Though take me not wrong. Cold nights call for warm sleeping. But enough of that. I go to Mercia to King Burghred and marry his daughter Godgifu. Happily for him—though not I fear for long—he has made compact with the Army of the Heathens and they leave him in peace, though he pay tribute still."

"Peace is not bought by geld."

"Aye, but Burghred has always sought the back way out of trouble. And it is not a matter for our present talk. These are bad times—but the House of Cerdic must be preserved—and that through the fruit of our loins. The skald singers rhyme of love and fair ladies sighing for lack of it. And pretty, too, 'tis to hear. But no more. The true line of royal blood is held only through marriage and a full quiver of sons to rise one by one and hold the line. Our father knew that."

"You speak nothing that I would gainsay."

"But now I do, perhaps. The ways of God are hidden from us. Life's battle is no less certain than a warrior's when the shield wall breaks. Death has its own commander. So to you I say with brotherly love and understanding—you have had your fill of wild oat sowing. The good book says it is better to marry than to burn. So I have chosen a bride in Mercia, too, for you."

Alfred laughed. "Such kindness. But does marriage bar a man from poaching a neighbour's does?" Then, seeing his brother's frown, he said soberly. "I jest. But now I listen plainly to you, my king, as a brother Cerdinga, and am at your command. Who is this lady—reasonably fair to look at, I hope?"

"So I am told. And one that our beloved mother would have welcomed."

"Our mother had kindness for everyone. But—go on and paint me the bright picture of the future."

"Her name is Elswitha, a modest and pleasant looking girl.

The daughter of Ethelred, Alderman of the Gainas, and Eadburgh, his wife."

"Small beer."

"The lady Eadburgh is of the blood royal of Mercia. And men do not call Ethelred the Muckle for nought. The thing is set and the times being what they are loins must fruit and the House of Cerdinga stand long after we are gone. So what say you?"

Alfred shrugged his shoulders. "I do as you wish because I honour and obey you as Head of the Cerdingas. But do not ask a man to change his nature."

His brother laughed. "All I ask from you is to take this woman for wife and bed her with honour and so widen the blood lines of the Cerdingas. These times are bloody and will be bloodier. There is no tree so well rooted that God's winds cannot topple it, though he spare the young saplings already shooting around it."

"Amen to that."

The King laughed again and said, "I will give you Amen for Amen. But though I am little older than you—you have much to learn, and learn you will, and the gods—"

"You go back a little in our ancestry, I think?"

"There is only one God and He has charity for any slip of the tongue. Old beliefs die hard. Do you not touch wood for good luck?"

Alfred grinned. "If I thought it would work I would touch the Devil's backside to get me what I want."

"Which is?"

"The day I know I will name it for you. Something moves me—unnameable, except that I do not think the destiny of man is forever battle. We take the shape of the life we know and fancy it is fixed. But we are deceived. We live on this earth and we long for Heaven. I think we do wrong. I think God's design ... aye, or the gods'—though quote me not to any high bishop—is still hidden. Maybe we ill maul this life while we wait for the pleasures of Paradise. Yet it is here, one day, that it waits for us ... just as once and so shortly Adam and Eve knew it in their garden. God is all goodness.

The day will come when the saints will walk this earth again with us."

"You talk wild. Which is safe with me. But guard your tongue and school your dreams—and wed the Alderman of the Gainas' daughter. Your mind is a muddied pond. Time will clear it."

"Amen. And I marry as you command and hope that the good Elswitha is well formed and her breath sweet." Then with a great laugh, he went on, "You think our horses understand our talk? And smile to themselves at man's foolishness knowing that life is but hard labour and happiness a warm stall and a full corn rack. No more no less?"

With his free hand the king crossed himself, and said, "Enjoy your wildness and blasphemy, brother. Time brings in strange changes."

*   *   *   *

That day, too, Oricson of Gerskat lay on a bed of coarse sacking stuffed with duck feathers and down, the work of his doxy Ina whom he had taken as warrior's right after the first sacking of York. Peace which was no true peace having been made with the coming of the winter months, he now shared quarters with the other warriors of the army of Guthrum on the banks of the river Humber. A sword slash, half parried in the fighting some months since, had long refused healing but was now—thanks to Ina's herbs and simples—giving true promise that when Guthrum with the coming of the fine weather turned his eyes northwards over the river to York he would be whole fighting man again.

Ina thrust aside the rough blanket of the door flap and came in carrying a wicker trug in which still jostled and raised armed claws her taking of crabs from the river pots she had set. Some rough provisioning there was for all the warriors from the Army levies on the countryside, but it was often little and each man filled his want from his own resources. Some shared slaves and some shared work willing women who after daylight labour made their beds warm and gave comfort. Ina was tall and dark and plain, but loving and pliant under the rough bed covers, and she kept his war gear clean and burnished and tended his healing with her simple skills so that he was now near whole man again. He had a gratitude to her which he seldom over-showed, but at which she guessed without the need of words.

She grinned at him and said, "The wind bites with the grip of a conger eel. I make fish soup and when the sun beds then so do we."

He smiled and gripped one of her buttocks tenderly and said, "You do all this for one of your country's enemies?"

"The answer to that you have had long since. This is a land where a woman has no safety and her only country is the small patch her man stands on. Tomorrow—you walk to the foreland and back. In a week—you sit a horse. And in a month your eyes will turn northwards with all your fellows."

"And you will follow me?"

"A woman like me can make no claim. But I will follow if that is your wish—until I can follow no longer."

"No longer? What words are those?"

"Are you so innocent, raven man, that you think children come from finding under a gorse bush?"

"You are with child?"

"Ask me that question in a month's time and I will give you true answer."

"You have your marsh herb skills."

"You think when the net is drawn there is not one fish that slips through the mesh? Now—I tell you that Rainar is outside."

"You stayed him there?"

"Aye—and had I found you sleeping well he would have come again."

"You act like a wife."

"Aye, and the acting holds some comfort—of which in these times there is much lack. You would I stay outside while you talk?"

"There is nought he can say to me of my country and people which needs keeping from you."

When Rainar, a short, thickset man wearing a sealskin helmet and wrapped in a long cloak, who could give Oricson more than a handful of years, came in Ina served them wild hop brew and then went about her cooking as they talked. Sometimes she lost their words' meanings but never so much as to be lost for a guess at their drift. Rainar was Oricson's closest friend and she knew that he had recently made a winter crossing back to his home country in one of the large dragon ships. Knew, too, that it was for the purpose of their great leader Guthrum who called for more ships and more men to help him tame her land and its people— which was nothing to raise her emotions for her land had never given her so much that she could grieve its loss. Men fought for land and power and took women and plunder as of right. A woman of sense accepted her lot and, if she could, submitted to the good Lord's will without lamentation. All she had ever needed was a man to stand before her against other men and so to serve him with all the wants he claimed from her, and to find contentment in so doing. Maybe if these sea-dragon men took this land there would be smoother times and no more burning of crops. Slave she was to her man's service and body and she was well content since before him there had been others who had treated her as less than their horses and hunting dogs. Aye, fine thanes and puffed up carls with rich yardlands ... geboors even and weorcmen. No woman alone was ever safe. Oricson was kind, except in drink or when his scramaseax or sword was still bloodied.

That night as they lay under their covers before sleeping, the dying fire embers deep shadowing their hut, she said, "Why did you laugh so much when Rainar told you of the woman Gerda?"

"'Tis a story too long to tell. Except that she has been sent away from Gerskat because a Saxon slave has put her with child—and yet knows it not."

"Your people will kill him for this?"

"No. There is to it that which I do not understand— except that in some way he has gained the favour of my father and a good man—Noth—our shipwright."

"And just that for so much laughter? It happens everywhere. Slave I am and may carry your child one day."

" 'Tis deeper than that—too deep for me to guess. But it is in my destiny that one day—since insult lies between us— we shall meet and only one will walk away whole from that meeting."

"You would fight a slave?"

"Why not if the gods have touched him for that purpose? Maybe the gods have touched you—since I find in you, slave as you are, a spirit that holds a freedom of mind which I should beat from any other woman. Now give me that which passes freely between us as man and woman and tomorrow you shall see me so restored that I will walk to the foreland point and back with you."

"I give you nothing on curt demand. You know the way to the flowering of that want without words."

"Aye, and so I do—and so I do now, my marsh girl. And there lies the god's touch that links us all for it comes to me that now you are drawn into my life for good reason."

"I lose you."

"Aye, in one way. But now you gain me. Lie still, marsh woman, and let me play the finger dance on your brown skin."

*   *   *   *

On a day when the mere ice could no longer be trusted and close to the base of the clumps of sered reed and rushes could be seen the first fingers of new growth show, the blocks were laid down in Noth's yard to take the keel of Justus's butterfly boat. For this keel there already lay under cover in the yard shed the stem and the stern of the boat, ready to be scarfed to it. Other sections of the craft lay, too, under cover, prepared through the long winter though not without argument and cross argument between Justus and Noth— though all this without heat.

But now after the laying of the keel on its blocks, Noth called to his workmen and, as they gathered round, he said

93

to Justus, "There is no happiness in a keel unless it can claim a name for the burden it shall bear. So—" he nodded to an upturned pork brining barrel on which stood a wine skin and drinking horns, "—you must name the craft so that it lies content to shoulder all burden you shall come to put on it."

Surprised, Justus said, "You ask me to name it?"

"Who else? Did it not spring from your butterfly brushed brain?"

The men around laughed as they filled their drinking horns for they knew by now the story of Justus's inspiration and also now well-liked him though none knew anything of the hidden compact between master and man.

Justus said, "You give me honour."

"Then name her well—for I have known craft take womanlike affront at a wrong name and never give good service. Name her, marshman, and we will drink fair winds and kind seas for her—though, by Odin, she will have to handle far worse."

Justus hesitated for a while, and then with a grin on his face said, "I would name her—Sea Otter."

"Why so?" asked Noth.

Justus grinned. "Because that creature knows only safety at sea. It lives and feeds there and, so 'tis said, at night turns on its back and sleeps safely in the roughest of waters."

" 'Tis well named and for good reason," said Noth, smiling.

So the drinking horns were filled and the craft's name toasted. At that moment, far away to the east in Hedeby, Gerda—sitting at her loom in the King's Lady's weaving room working her shuttle on a half-finished length of diagonally patterned twill cloth to make a summer cloak for the King—felt the child within her kick hard as though there were a growing impatience in it for escape. Although she knew nothing of Noth's compact with Justus the wish was in her that when it came it would be a man child, and more that it could have been the child of her long lost battle-killed lover. For herself she would have wished to have stayed in Gerskat and borne the child. She would have made no claim on Justus

94

and, although people would have talked, there was always a short season to such incidents, and many a Gerskat girl in the past would have been hard put to give right name to the father of her child.

One of her companions came into the room and stood for a while behind her, watching her work and then, with a long sigh, turned away and stared out of the unshuttered window at the bright waters of the river estuary and said, "I would I had your skills—and so could find forgetfulness in work."

"Why so?"

"Because there are times when the men are away that the not-knowing of their doings is a black itch in the mind. Twice I have been loved and promised, and twice I have watched the war-craft come riding up the estuary on the tide and seen another man at the oar bench which held the one I loved when the hands were raised in parting."

"The gods give and the gods take—and women's hearts are with time schooled to sorrow."

"Not so mine. Now I have shut it away where no man can ever truly again touch it. My body is for lease, but never again my heart." She turned suddenly and smiled. "Some time I will make a song for my feeling."

*   *   *   *

Midway between Pentecost and Midsummer's Day the *Sea Otter* was finished and her first trials under sail had been carried out and proved equal to the demands which Noth had insisted should be answered. On the evening of a day when a stiff south-westerly wind blew, and a high sea came roaring into the Gerskat river mouth, Noth had watched Justus take her down river and out into the spume-crested waves of the estuary. When she had rounded the point and become lost to sight, he had sat and waited while the sun dipped lower in the sky and the tide ran out.

He waited, unmoving, his eyes on the river mouth, while the sun dropped reddening down the sky and there was in him neither hope nor despair. The iron clamp of coming loss was already on him. The *Sea Otter* would not fail him or Justus. Between them they had given too much of themselves and their craft not to know that it would—with a little favour from the gods—answer all Justus's demands. Neither had Gerda failed him for news had lately come that she had been delivered of a healthy son. Pray the gods be kind, he thought, and gift son like father.

He waited until the dusk brought out the first of the pipistrelle bats from the ship loft roof to begin their evening's hawking, and then saw the *Sea Otter* round the far point of the river mouth and come riding in on the long rise and fall of the sea-swollen tide, and watched with a sad lift of pride how the craft moved and with more pride as off the boat slip Justus from his stern seat leaned forward and slacked the hoist yard and the butterfly sail came down, flapping and shaking and was loose furled to its boom as Justus brought the craft head up into the wind and tide and then with a short oar paddled her into the foot of the slip.

Noth went down and held her bows while Justus jumped overboard into the shallow water. Together they ran her up the log roller slip until she was clear of the river. The water on her bottom boards slid back to the stern and, seeing Noth's eyes on it, Justus, smiling happily, his eyes bright with the confidence which inhabited him, said, "At no time while I have been out have I used the baling scoop so that you would see how little she had shipped water. She answers all that I ask of her."

Noth nodded, and then said, "Bale her out now and stow the sail right. Then come to me in the loft." He walked away, feeling age and sadness drag heavily on him.

When Justus eventually came to him he had set out two mugs of wine on the small table at Justus's bedside.

As Justus sat on the side of his bed, Noth said, jerking his head towards the day-marking stick which lay on the bed, "Cut today's notch a long one. You are free to go at any time of your choosing. But name me not the day nor give me any sign of its coming. This you will know well how to arrange. I say this because your going to freedom is a matter between myself and Oric. What the workmen and the Gerskat people may come to think is of no matter."

"I will settle it so. And ask no question of you why I have your kindness and that of Oric. You have treated me like father and—for Oric, I could wish there were no bad blood between me and his son. For you, too, I wish there were more I could leave you than my words of gratitude for your kindness. I shall go soon. And, since Gerda is not here, I would you will give her my thanks for her kindness and goodness to me. Our different people make war. That is God's will—and no man can seek to find His reasoning except that from all suffering sooner or later comes great good, though this, I fancy, long after our times."

Noth grinned unexpectedly, and said, "When you need you have a smooth tongue. Save that skill to calm the waters." Noth raised his wine beaker. "I wish you a fair and a safe passage."

"And for you long years and many more keels to lay."

Two weeks later, some time after midnight and under a clouded sky that hid the moon and as the first of the tide began to run out, Justus ran the *Sea Otter* down the slip to the river, took the pair of short oars and went down stream. At the mouth of the river he ran the boat ashore at the beginning of the sand dunes.

From the dunes, where he had hidden them on several night forays, he gathered up his waterskins and his provisions of dried meat and fish and store of hard-baked barley bread. With all safely stowed aboard he pushed the *Sea Otter* free from the land and then hauled himself aboard. The tide took him and, as the sail was hauled up the wind filled it gently and the boat's bows swung towards the open sea, reaching to the south-west and in his mind ran the first of the sailing directions given him by Noth—*a full day's sailing south by west for two days . . .*

*　　*　　*　　*

The Atheling Alfred went into his new wife's chamber. Elswitha was sitting at the open window, a loose shawl around her shoulders over her night shift as she braided her long hair. She turned and smiled at him, a pleasant to near good-looking young woman with whom he was well content for she was an amiable, compliant creature who met all his demands with more than simple wifely obedience—a woman, too, he gave thanks for. Since her coming he had kept only to her bed and prayed that with God's good grace it would stay so. Though when she should come to be big with child—for which he prayed, partly for himself and partly for the good of the House of Cerdic—he would, he knew, at times need to ease the robust passions of his flesh elsewhere, knowing that he would have her understanding. There was a simplicity and generosity about her which touched him deeply.

She said, "My lord—I thought you had ridden for Winchester this day?"

"And so had I thought to. But my brother, the king, sends word for me and my men to ride to join him at Wantage."

"Why so?"

"I could wish that the *why* were a good one. But 'tis not so. Word has come from Burghred, king of the Mercians, praying for help from my brother, the king, and of all the fighting men of the West Saxons."

Elswitha's hands fell from a half-braided tress of hair. "What moves with the king to make such a call?"

"That which is never content unless it is always moving seeking plunder and pillage. The Heathen Army turns away from York and Northumbria and begins to move into Mercia against Burghred at Nottingham. Already the word has gone out and my brother's fyrds begin to gather."

Elswitha raised a forefinger to her mouth and bit at it gently in her concern, then said, "I would that you were not going—and I would not that you do other than you do."

Alfred laughed. "Almost you make a riddle of your *would* and your *would not*. Would and would not—the two tides of men's lives."

"Aye—and the burden of all women's. For being weak they can but sit at home and offer no more than prayer."

Alfred smiled. "I understand you. But you are wrong with your 'no more'. There is a power in prayer which is God's shield for a man. I would never go into battle without it. Nor my brother, the king—though I have to mark that he makes his prayers long while I keep mine short. So I am here to bid you finish your braiding soon for I would have you and your ladies ride to Wantage with my party."

"Why so, my lord?"

He grinned and let a hand slide inside the neck of her bed robe, caressing her breast gently as he bent and kissed her lips. Then standing back, he said, "There is your answer. We shall be some time at Wantage while the fyrds are gathered—and overmuch grumbling there will be since it is near harvest time. Winter for war, and summer for the tending of crops and harvesting. All things have their season —except with the Heathen for in this land they sow not but only reap other men's harvests. Though it is said that there be some in the Eastlands of Anglia who have turned husbandmen. So, my Elswitha—it is Wantage for you and your ladies until my brother has gathered his warriors."

"I would go with you to Mercia."

"No. Why—your folk might think that you long for your old home because here I ill-treat you and tire of you."

"My lord, you are all caring."

"Aye, so I find. And it pleases me beyond telling. There is a folly in thinking the fruit in another man's garth is fairer than the fruit in your own. Now I go and leave you to call your ladies and make ready."

Leaving her he went down into the palace yard and in a few moments had forgotten her in his war business with the gathering of the first of the aldermen and thanes who had arrived with their fyrd men—these last, many of them with their own yardlands, far from pleased at crops left to be ungathered and spoiled. The Devil take the Heathens who had no respect for seasons.

99

4

A FAIR WIND had favoured Justus for five days, the sun
had shone down on him from an almost cloudless sky and at
night the full moon waning to its last quarter had silvered
the easy running swell of the sea. With the rising of the sun
each morning he greeted it with prayer and with its setting
at night he saluted its going with thanksgiving for that day's
smooth passage. For sleep, he took it when he could no
longer resist its power, lowering the sail and then streaming
from the bows a stout ox-skin drogue so that the *Sea Otter*
headed up into the run of the sea and the full face of the
wind. For company he sometimes had a school of porpoises,
sometimes a lone gull that hovered over his wake as he had
seen such birds do astern of the *Fafnir* in the days of his
taking, wheeling and crying and waiting for the garbage
scraps. There was little that he could spare, but from
superstition he always found a few hard crust edges of wheat
loaf to gift to the birds. Once distantly he had marked the
great square sail of a Heathen warcraft and he had changed
course to take the *Sea Otter* well away from it before he could
be seen.

On his third day he had set his course due west and late
in the afternoon had marked far distant ahead of him the
low line of land. For safety he altered course to take him
away from land for he had no wish to make a landing on the
East coast of his country.

Sometimes he found himself wondering what mystery there
could be that lay behind the final kindness of Noth in making
his freedom possible. Sometimes, too, he found himself
talking aloud as though he were already safely back in his

own land and answering the folk questions of his crossing and the building of the *Sea Otter*, and there was now and then a growing arrogance in him as fancy turned to fact in his imagination, and that fact moved him to boastfulness. He had come from the land of the Heathens by the use of his own powers and skills and—surely?—the blessing of the good Lord on him. There was God's work waiting ahead of him to be done. Aye, and that work plain. To take sword against the Heathen men.

Sometimes there was a sadness and misery in him. In his marshland home he had known happiness, and seen greater happiness ahead with Riada denied him. God then, surely, had taken all that from him for a better and harder purpose. God must be with him, like a good father, guiding and shaping his destiny. So be it, since there was no gainsaying it. God had His reasons, and no man could search them through to an end—only by living his days as they came would understanding grow. But the bold shape was now true. The Heathen men had come to take his land, and the Heathen men were there now, and if the good Lord gave him safe passage he knew what he must do—unless the Lord gave him other sign—and that was to take mailed brynie, leather fighting cap, a sword to be sand scoured to brightness that would dazzle a man's eyes, and to be fine edged and pointed to find Heathen flesh and bone—aye, and a stout shield which he would make for himself and paint boldly on it the bloody cross of the Saviour. For all this, he was sure, God gave him now fair wind. And soon now must come the moment when he could turn the *Sea Otter*'s bows westwards and find land running with him on the steerboard side.

Three days later, on a day of a high raging summer gale, a party of monks, riding the long line of sands on the Kentish Wealden coast, whipped sea spume blowing across the dunes, sand grains biting into their faces, came across the splintered and rock shattered bow section of the *Sea Otter*, which they took to be the wreckage of some fisherman's craft. Eager to reach their minster and comfort after a long journey, they rode on. Each crossed himself and, dutifully, mumbled some brief prayer for the soul of any fisherman who might have gone drowning to the Good Lord, and then spat wind-whipped sand grains from dry mouths.

*　　*　　*　　*

Riada's second child—a boy—was born at Winchester where Arnulf had gone to become master of the great minster's masons and to supervise the work of re-roofing the nave, which had fallen into disrepair. He was now a man of importance with his own wooden lodge on the outskirts of the city, a lodge which he planned some time to pull down and rebuild in stone and, on the slight fall of ground to the river, to set out a herb and flower garden and a plot of vines so that in time they might make their own wine. With his rise in the world he had become a little pompous and sharp with his workmen, about which Riada sometimes teased him—but in her heart she was proud of his rising importance and knew that with it there was no escaping the need to be seen and heard to be master. Though she knew well that the change was also justified for many of his men were young and high-spirited and, though they raised monuments to God and kept His house in good state, when the wine or the Devil was in them their tongues were loose with oaths and their dusty throats often well slaked with ale and mead ... aye, and the monks' wine if chance came their way.

When he stepped back from the bed where she lay with the new child swaddled and held close to her, he smiled and said "This day you have given me great joy—and there is no doubt that I shall make you and our children proud of me. The bishop himself, I know, will christen him—for I already have his promise." He grinned, and added, "A good craftsman is not only worthy of his hire—but also of a few graces which not all men can claim. One day, you will see, you shall have silks and rare stuffs to your fair body ... and shall drink from silver cups ... aye, or maybe rare coloured glass goblets which the traders bring from the lands of the Great Middle Sea. Aye, and—"

"Aye, and—" Riada interrupted him with a smile, "—that I would enjoy but less for my own pleasure than yours. With you I need neither good nor bad fortune. My need is you alone. And so—what name would you have for this son of yours?"

"Of that I must think. The naming of a boy is a serious matter—for often, as the grain runs in a stone and shows the way to its shaping, so it is with a child's name. Bad or hurriedly name it and harm can be done. I shall ask the bishop for the favour of his counsel."

"You do that, Master Arnulf—and do not think that I am lost to the fact that you tease me a little. Nor that I think you without a certain slyness when you make your way so warmly with the bishop. Good man he is—but good man you would have him be to you and so you solemn your voice to him and bow your head. Sometimes perhaps to hide a little smile at your cunning?"

"As my master I give him every respect. But he is man, too—and like a good stone must be worked the proper way of the grain. And for you, you are too sharp not to read me— and to my delight I find it pleases me. Another man would beat you for your forwardness." He reached out and taking her free hand kissed it, and then said, "But remember this, and I swear it in honour of you, little Otta is first born in this house and stands next to me always as god-gifted. That was God's will and I gladly embrace it. Now I go to take supper with my men so that they can drink to my good fortune. But if you have need send your serving woman to call me."

When he was gone Riada lay back on her bed, cradling her child. From the room below she could hear the sound of her servant girl chattering away to young Otta who now could walk and crawl his way into mischief and chatter back to the girl in his own broken language, and hearing Otta she more than spared thought of long-lost Justus ... though now with a calm acceptance of that distant loss. The shaping of God's will was sometimes sharp to accept, but by His goodness there came in the end calm acceptance of a design to each of the sorrows that fell upon His people. Justus no longer lived for her. The weeks and months and years had taken him from her and hope, like a green leaf, had withered slowly and finally fallen to ground to crumble into dust. Memory remained but the heart's ache like mist under the sun had died away. *His will be done* ... She and little Otta were Arnulf's and she thanked the good Lord for that strong comfort.

For the first time since she had known him Arnulf came back drunk that night. Wrapped in an old wolf-skin robe he slept on dusty planks in his garden workshop, but on the verge of sleep muttered to himself that there were times when a man must accept temptation and Adam's lot. Drunk he was and with no regrets for he was now true father ... God be praised—and help him to get through the next day's work without shaming himself ...

* * * *

Towards the end of that year, 868, King Ethelred and his brother, Alfred the Atheling, returned from Mercia in low spirits and disappointment for the Heathen Army had fortified themselves in the citadel at Nottingham and refused to sally forth and give battle, and so sat secure against the not over-spirited sallies which King Burghred and his Wessex allies made. Peace—which neither side saw as being for long —was made between the Mercians and the Heathen commanders, and tribute made to them by King Burghred.

Riding back with his king brother at the head of their fyrds and not unhappy levies, Alfred said, "It seems that the pattern of the Danes changes. They seek now to sit as though by right in Northumbria and Mercia. Fight they will in part when they cannot force tribute by arms. But, I fancy, there is another yeast working in them—"

"Aye, because beyond fighting and battle they now seek more than mere plunder and tribute. Land and crops and cattle ... and for these why spill blood when weak men like Burghred will pay them to stay their sword arms? The days of their pirate raids when the raven's wind brought them for summer pillaging are fast dying. Conquest is the prize—and they play that game now by the cozenage of such weak men as Burghred. He will rue this autumn's cowardice. In the years to come Mercia will fall to them ... aye, and all the land of the East Saxons. Peace is not bought with gold."

"And when the lands of the East Saxons and Mercians finally come to their hand and their peoples accept heathen overlordship—what then, my brother?"

Ethelred drew deep breath and then fell into a fit of coughing as the growing frost of the dying day touched his throat. Recovering, he wrapped his scarlet riding cloak closer about him and said sharply, "You need me to read that riddle for you? Each alderman and thane that rides behind us ... aye, and each yeoman and his workmen—they know the answer. And why should they not? Our forefathers, long years ago, did what the Danes seek to do now. Times change but the pattern follows its true shape untouched by the years. Next year or the year beyond will come the turn of all the Wessex lands. A man with the fire of lust in his veins seeks a woman. But a man with the raw greed of land hunger carries a passion for possession which is almost next to holiness."

"Or devilry?"

"The two mark the same coin. Spin it and it matters not which side faces the day's light." He laughed suddenly, and then went on, "They will come, my brother—if not in my time then in yours. So then, we must use our days to make ready for their coming. The house of Cerdic must stand. Two duties we have. Male heirs from our wives and the spreading of the word through all the Wessex lands to sharpen each alderman, thane and yeoman to this knowledge. So I give you charge this winter—" he grinned, "since you take hard riding in winter so lightly—to go to all our people from Canterbury east first and then west to Exeter.

Paint them all the picture in its true colours and see that when you leave them they will know that they must stand ever sharp and ready for the coming storm."

Alfred laughed. "My thanks, brother—Since this winter, so all the old men tell, promises to be harder than any for years past."

So it was that a week before All Saints day Alfred with his small travelling household band found himself in Canterbury lodged in the palace of Archbishop Ceolnoth, making known to that good man the run of the future as his brother had seen it and calling on him to have each priest and monk in his lands to speak the warning of his brother, and to call gatherings of aldermen and thanes to ready them against the danger which King Ethelred had marked in the future.

They sat in a small and simple room which overlooked the close. A fire burned in the open grate and, now and then, as the winter wind gusted outside, smoke blew back into the room and made the old man cough, though there was a merry twinkle in his faded blue eyes as he observed, "So it is said with truth—there is no smoke without fire. And rightly. So you come to tell me of the rising smoke that foretells the Heathen fire? The King's warning I will make known— though he under-rates the good sense of my countrymen here. They have lived closer to the Heathen on Thanet than most for many a year—but to deny the proverb that familiarity breeds contempt, there is no man in these lands who does not know and dread the peril which lurks outside our doors."

"Aye, good father, I know. But now it must be known that all good men should be ready to ride and fight in the protection of all Wessex peoples. One twig snaps easily. Bind them and there is defiance of the strongest hands. God helps those who help others."

The old man chuckled. "Atheling and future king you are, my son—but a good priest is lost in you somewhere." He dropped a thin hand on the manuscript book which lay open on his knees and went on, "You read the good words of Our Lord and the lives of our blessed saints and scholars?"

106

Alfred shrugged his shoulders, "No, my lord, I cannot read. But I have a memory that hoards away all I hear or have read to me. *Miserere mihi, Domine, et exaudi orationem meam ...*"

The Archbishop chuckled, raised a hand briefly in blessing, and said, "I pray God that one day in your time there will come the days when you can turn from your royal duties and find the peace to discover that the Word is stronger than the sword which must fall into rust. In some part the heathen Danes are here to stay. But they are God's children even though they know it not ... Time and God's truth outlive all the world's days. I would say to you—" He stopped suddenly and laughed briefly and then went on, "I grow old. Here you come with true warrior concern for your country and need not my preaching. Now, I say, I will call the gathering you need. And also, since I hear that, a few days since, you have lost your personal man servant from the fever that gathers in this land, I will make you gift of one to serve you and follow you for the rest of your days. He is a man of low birth, but of good sense and courage. Aye, and godly in his own way."

"You are kind, my lord. But there is no call for such a kindness I can—"

"I gift him to you for I think you will find him more than servant. His name is Justus—and he lives with one desire in him—to take arms and service against the Heathen Danes. One night, when sleep escapes, you should hear his story."

Alfred gave a little shrug of his shoulders and smiled. The good Archbishop was old and kind and not to be gainsaid for that would be to lack courtesy. He said, "I thank you, my lord."

Early that evening, when Alfred came back to his room after talking to the Alderman of Canterbury on the same matter but in blunter words than he had used with the Archbishop, he found his newly gifted servant waiting for him. A fire burned brightly in his room and a glance showed him that his travelling pack had been unstrapped and his clothes and personal gear laid out neatly on a long side table.

With it were a fine Venetian jug holding wine and a golden goblet whose worth would have bought enough land to set a man up with his own yardlands and enough over for seed to sow it and oxen to plough it.

Still a little unsettled at the way the Archbishop had placed the man with him, he said shortly, "You are Justus?"

"I am, my lord."

"And now gifted to me by the good Ceolnoth."

For a moment or two Justus made no reply, but stood silently eyeing the young atheling who, with a swift rise of irritation said, "Did you lose your tongue when you gained that scar on your face?"

"No, my lord. And, if you do not wish my service I will go since I know that no prince wishes to have his personal servant chosen for him. The good Archbishop is old and over-impetuous to please those whom he loves since his time runs short for such acts."

"By the sword, you have an easy tongue. But learn this —a gift from the holy Ceolnoth is not to be rejected unless time proves such of no worth. Where got you that scar on your face?"

"I am a marshman from the Athelney fens, my lord. Near three years ago I was taken from there by the men of a Heathen dragon ship and so to their own lands to be slave. Not long since I escaped in a small boat which was wrecked off the Wealden coast where a party of good monks found me lying for dead on the shore—"

Alfred laughed disbelievingly. "And they brought you here where your ready tongue ... aye, and a saucy one ... charmed the good Ceolnoth whom it is known will swallow any wild tale of miracles." Then, his face darkening, he went on, "Get you out from here. I have campaigned enough to fend for myself when needs be. Go! I am in no mood for old wives' tales of the impossible."

"As you wish, my lord."

Justus bowed his head and left the room. With the man gone, sensible that he had perhaps spoken over-sharply since, though the man hawked a fanciful tale he had held himself well and with more than a common dignity, Alfred touched by some stir of conscience went to the table and filled the goblet with wine which he drank rapidly knowing that it would ease the bite of pain in his groin which had set hard on him during the fruitless time spent in Mercia.

That evening, as he ate with the Archbishop and his priests in the good man's palace, the wine and fine food moving him to comfort of body, he enquired of Ceolnoth's chaplain the true history of the man Justus.

The chaplain smiled at him, and said, "You think he is impostor, my lord, with a smooth tongue to charm his way into my lord's favour?"

"What else? Children love such tales ... and with loyal respect for Ceolnoth, so do men in their wintering when there are but few sered leaves left to fall from the tree of their life."

The chaplain put down the leg of plump fowl he was eating, wiped his mouth fat free with the back of his hand, and said, "The world is full of miracles ... some small, some large. Some of ready import and some that take years to come to recognition. But here, my lord, is no miracle. And I would save you from sorrowing Ceolnoth by disdaining his offering to you."

"What? Has this marshman rogue charmed you all with his tale?"

"There was no need, my lord. I was there on the shore at the time. The weather was wild and we came across the fore part of the wrecked boat on the beach, and then some way beyond there was this marshman countryman of ours, near naked, bloodied and like dead."

Alfred laughed with a whisper of scorn in his voice still, and said, "So—he told you this tale and you believed it? A fishing marshman ... soft-talking your hearts?"

"Charity came first. We gave it and saved his life. But I was as you. The next morning when Justus had told his tale I commanded the yeoman whose lands run down to that shore to have what remained of Justus's craft wagon-lifted here where those who know such things say that no such ship-craft work is known here in the shaping of small boats. Justus spoke truth, and since then has told full story of his captivity."

The next morning Alfred sent for Justus and, since he was a man of good faith and frank to confess his own short-comings, he said directly, "I have done you wrong—and freely confess it since the good priest who was with the party that found you has told me all your story. Later, I wish to go and see what remains of your boat, and then to hear your story from your own lips. I spoke hastily and do recall my words, and would have you in my service. But this I say, too—I charge you to stand free and, if it is your wish, to refuse my service." He paused a moment or two, and then went on, "I see you part smile. Why so?"

"Why, from happiness, my lord. Last eve I was cast down in my desires. This morn I stand happy. I am free man. All I wish to do is to serve you against the Heathens."

"And so you shall and ride with me when the times come. As for your tale, since I have much to do here and in all the Wessex lands, you will give it to me as it comes ... day by day and—" Alfred grinned, "—if you paint your story too bright or fierce a colour take no heed since you will be in good company. Songs and tales grow and take over ever brighter or blacker colour in the telling and re-telling. That is the law which makes legends. So marshman, you have had a prince take back his words to you. Tell that, too, sometime to your children. History lives from mouth to mouth. The good clerics can get but little of it into their manuscripts."

So, Justus, through what he knew must be miracle, entered the service of the House of Cerdic and of Alfred, the Atheling, who stood next in line to the kingship. And his happiness over-rode the black memory of the loss of the *Sea Otter* when after days of calm and good winds, the sea and its storms had turned against him and driven him on to shore rocks which tore the heart from his craft and near drowned him as he lay bleeding and half-dead from a blow of the mast as it was torn from its keelson.

*   *   *   *

That winter and into the Spring of the year 869, while Alfred and his company travelled the length of all Wessex, a different enemy came to the country for plague began to run through all its lands and there was a great failing of all the Spring seedings while the previous year's harvest grains and roots rotted in their sacks and clamps. Men dropped from life as they walked, milk dried to make mothers' breasts barren, and over the roads and footways a sky gathering of ravens and eagles marked the place of travellers' corpses, and the wolves and foxes grew fat and bold, taking the weak and stumbling even in the night dark of the towns and villages. In Mercia the Heathen Army moved away from Nottingham and went north to York and made a great camp there where the famine and plague raged less strongly.

It was at York as the first primroses began to fade and the cuckoo birds called all day that Weyn, a newly arrived Dane from Hedeby, came to the small quarters Oricson had in the unburnt part of a thane's house where he lived with Ina.

Towards the end of their talk, he said, "And you should know, too, that your friend, the Saxon marshman—with whom you have blood feud—has gone from Gerskat some long time ago ..." He told the story such as he knew it—that rumour said Noth had had part in the escape, and even that his own father had held back from standing in the way, though it was rumoured that he had been privy to the whole affair.

"I care not," said Oricson. "Behind it all stand the gods. The marshman will be in his own country even though his craft were destroyed. The gods will have lent him webbed feet until he touched shore." He called to Ina to bring them Frankish wine, and went on. "He will be in his own Wessex and the talk is now that these parts get too settled, the Saxon folk submit and pay tribute, and our fighting men rot with lack of action. So soon, you will see, we shall turn south and west and sword and axe will no longer rust from want of use. These parts are done. They whine but they pay their geld and herd their cattle for us. I tease my mind with the insult the marshman would return for mine. I care not how small or large it is. The gods have surely marked it for saying one day."

"And who," said Ina sharply, "have your gods marked for dying that day?"

Oricson laughed. "You seek to know the future? Stay that kind of thought. What will be will be." Then turning back to Weyn he said, "And what other news from Gerskat?"

"Little—though there was talk that your father may this year sail the new *Fafnir* and his men to the land of the Franks where dragon ships and an army gather and there is great talk, too, of moving up the Seine to take Paris."

Oricson laughed. "I wish them well—but it will be a long haul against the stream. Noth will take no pleasure in that."

"Noth stays at Gerskat. His days at the steer-oar are finished for he has found other contentment."

"Why so?"

"Gerda has returned from Hedeby with a young colt at foot and although the father is not named his name is no mystery."

Oricson laughed. "Aye—that reads straight. So the marshman gifted old Noth with a great grandson. And what says Noth of that?"

"Nought—but the boy is the apple of his eye and already tumbles about the yard and cuts his teeth on rowlock pegs. Master shipwright Noth would make him and, since all love Noth, then all hope that he will have the length of years to see it come true."

"And *aye* I say to that, too." Oricson turned to Ina. "You hear that? Now find some old witch with simples and spells and gift me with son. It would be no more than fair handling between the Saxon and myself. By Odin's wounds, if the world turns like this then the leaven will spread and all men will be brothers in blood and all the lands at peace ... though," he grinned, "I would not live to see it so. I like too well the way the world turns now." He laughed aloud suddenly, thumping his fists on his knees, and almost shouted,

"By all the gods, there is something to send a man to Valhalla with. I begin to read the runes of the truce between Noth and my father. Justus gifted Noth without knowing it and Noth bound my father to his own will and so let him go knowing nothing of the child. But I will be kind to him when the meeting comes—before he dies I shall tell him of his bastard brat ..."

Ina laughed, tilting the wine skin to fill their drinking horns, and said slyly, "Aye—but good Oricson your gods may play cold tricks and it might be you that lengthed the ground with your life passing. Would you waste your last words to mock another?"

Undisturbed Oricson shrugged his shoulders and said, "Let that day and that destiny come if the gods so shape it. With the moment I will find answer." He stood up and reached for his sword belt and began to arm himself and said to Weyn, "I go to guard duty now but you stay. I gift Ina to you until I return. School her to know that a craft that carries too much sail in a high wind will capsize."

Her eyes suddenly blazing with anger Ina cried sharply, "Aye, let that be if it is your wish—but know that if it passes then there can be no night when you sleep in my arms that you can have sure knowledge of ever awakening."

Oricson laughed and said, "You see, Weyn, what a spitfire I take to bed? Well, will you have her—my gift stands?"

Weyn shook his head. "I would have her. What man would not? But I do not lack such comfort." Then turning to Ina he went on, "You are true to him and he knows it. Now let the matter die. I will come with you, Oricson."

"So be it." Then turning to Ina, Oricson laid the flat of a hand against her cheek kindly, and said, "I did but jest a little roughly. Drop the door bar after our going for you should know that I would gut the belly of any man who touched you."

"Let that be truth. I will have hare broth waiting for you. But know this—for our comfort—make not that kind of rough jest again."

"Nor will I ever. And when my sword arm weakens we

will take land here, stock it with fine cattle and horses, and seed it to fat cropping. I like this country and when the battle fever is done I would keep to it for ever."

*   *   *   *

During all the forepart of that year, 869, too, Justus travelled with the Atheling Alfred and learned quickly his duties and his place. They went through all the West Saxon lands and rough- or smooth-talked aldermen and thanes who made promises with no great heart for the land was in despair from plague and part famine. At times Alfred's band lay rough at nights when storm and bad going found them far from warm lodging or some thane's hall. Only when they reached the towns was there good lodging and comfort. One day, eating hard tack and drinking sour wine on the westerly edges of Ashdown forest, Alfred, in good mood (and Justus had quickly learned that he was a man of everchanging moods, sometimes full of laughter—bawdy and light—and sometimes, as though some inner blackness of spirit possessed him, a man for whom each word had to be weighed unless hidden offence goaded him to rage), took a stick and drew for him the rough outline of their land as far north in the east as Bamburgh and as far west as the isle of Anglesey. This was a matter of some excitement for Justus because he had lived all his years without any picture in his mind of the true shape of his country. On the map Alfred drew the boundaries of the Saxon domains and made crosses to mark the towns—a string of names which were to become known places, Basing, Reading, Malmesbury, Chippenham, Winchester, Shaftesbury, Sherborne, Chichester, Wimborne, Wareham, and far west his own Athelney and Exeter—and he traced in some of the rivers and the run of the old Roman roads still in use.

Then Alfred handed the stick to Justus and said, "Now draw me in its proper place the length and breadth of the Danes' country and the towns you knew or heard of there."

Justus did this as well as he was able and marked those

towns which he had heard of from Noth. From that he was bidden to go on and give the story of his boat building and journey to England, finishing with the tale of how, a day after sighting the first Channel run of his own country, a fierce wind and sea had risen and swamped the *Sea Otter* and he had been washed overboard and left to God's mercy—which, be praised, had been forthcoming.

After the telling Alfred sat for a while in silence and then said, "There are some things I wish to know. You have kin living?"

"If she still lives—a mother in my own marshland, my lord."

"When we go west you shall seek her out."

"You are kind, my lord."

"And you say that in their own land these Danes ... these Heathens—they are honest labourers and farmers, good husbands and fathers?"

"As near to any in our lands."

"Aye, that is something that I know, too, for I have travelled, though young, twice to Rome. Why then do you think that first my forefathers and now the Heathen men turned envious eyes towards these shores?"

"From hunger, my lord. Land hunger. Poor land, and too many mouths to feed, breed the lust to take other people's pastures."

"You have a gift in your hands, but in your tongue, too. Marshland may have bred you, but the good Lord must have touched you at birth. Now smooth-tongued one—is a rich island like this always so to be plagued?"

"I have no gift to see the future, my lord, but in my heart I read the answer. Yes."

"Then how are we and those that follow us to hold ourselves safe?"

Justus was silent for a while and then said, "I am not one to give you counsel, my lord. There are those more highly placed and fitted to answer you that."

Alfred spat angrily to the ground and said, "I made question of you. Answer—for I believe you were God-sent though you know it not. Why should he choose alderman or thane since he knows they all give the answer which they hope will best please me? There is always more flattery than truth in it. Now—you upstart marshman whose plain speech from any other man I would meed with a flogging—speak your mind."

"Since you ask it, my lord. In my sailing from Gerskat I thought of many things to wear the hours away. And sometimes fancied that I heard voices talk to me, and sometimes, though my eyes were open, I saw not the seas around me— but dream things that made my skin to creep."

"You make heavy weather of it. But I am patient since there is no hurry in me to sit my sore backside to saddle and ride yet. So speak frankly."

"Then I do, my lord. Those who live on an island live in a fortress whose walls are the sea. So, my lord, you must command those walls. You must have fighting ships to stop the Heathen pirates as they come. And those ships should be spread in good numbers at chosen ports along our coasts with their crews always ready to meet a call to battle. Just as, so I have heard, the Romans built a wall, coast to coast in the north of this island with forts at regular intervals."

"Aye, that rings true. But not all can be stopped. Come they will for God would send us defeats as well as victories at sea."

"I have no answer to that," said Justus faintly.

Alfred laughed. "Frankly spoken. But I have and will tell it you since what you say about victories at sea rings true. But you will keep closed mouth about it for its shape will please few. Yet done it must be. And, by the good Lord, there is something sparked in talking to you that brightens the days ahead for me. We make battle in winter since all the men of our fyrds have crafts to follow or crops to sow and reap and store. The heathen follows no such season—for he takes others' crops and cattle at will. But I would—*and will*—have it differently. I would have the fyrds levies split into winter and summer fyrds when I am king. And both at call if at any time the danger grow too great. It is rough division and

116

rude demand, but it must be. But this you will keep to yourself. Now, tell me something of the way the Heathen craftsmen work timber and shape their craft—nay, on second thought, we will leave that to another time for there is little enough left of the day to take us in good light to Basing."

From that day and from that talk between master and man a firmly shaped friendship grew between the two, but it was a friendship seldom openly marked in company for the Atheling Alfred was quick to show displeasure for any man who outstepped his position.

From time to time Alfred's progress was broken by returns to the King to give reports of his work and to attend to other state matters and also to be with his wife.

On one of these occasions he gave leave to Justus to ride back to his marshlands in search of his friends, but it was a sad return over which he did not linger. His mother was dead and from Riada's parents he learned that she had married Arnulf and lived following him in his work so that they got little news of her.

So Justus went back to Wilton where Alfred was lodged with the court and took up his duties and was not surprised—though the Atheling never mentioned it to him—when Paternus, the master of the Atheling's guard, came to him one day as he drank ale at evening in the servants' hall, and said, grinning, "Master Justus, I have been ordered to take you under my old and moulting wing. We do not say by whom. So, you webbed-footed marsh miracle man, I am to make a warrior out of you. Tomorrow you come to the armoury with me and, to begin with, I will deck you out to look like if not yet to be a fighting man. Broad sword, byrnie, round shield and helmet. And, by hell's fire, take care you turn out as ready with your arms as with your tongue. I shall make you sweat and ache and, to show it no shadow play, as near pass my blade to your throat or belly that there be only the thinness of a fish scale between you and death. You are content?"

Justus grinned. "Aye—you do that master, and the first Heathen I kill I will dedicate to you."

"Dedicate—what kind of Kate is that—not that whore who keeps the ale-house in the town's stews? Kate or dedicate, I will make fighting man of you. And read me not wrong —if you should slip or falter and perchance fall on my sword thrust and so spill your guts, I will see you decently buried."

"Thank you, master—and should the sword play turn roundabout—then I will do the same for you. Though with sorrow—for I would that the first man I kill be one of the Heathen men."

"Rush not, rush not—and for first thing, remember this, they fight like men and fiends, so never bend to spit in the face of one you have killed for they have all the tricks and it pleases them to go to their heathen Valhalla laughing over the stupidity of a cozened Saxon. And when I say tomorrow at the armoury I mean at first sparrow fart." Then, with a swift movement, the guard master drew the dagger from his belt and his arm went up to feign a blow at Justus's throat, but before the mock thrust could come Justus kicked Paternus's legs from him and he fell back to land sprawling on his backside.

For a moment or two the guard master lay there. Then slowly a grin spread over his weather-hardened cheeks and he sat up and pulled at his beard, saying, "Well, well ... 'twas goodly done. But not fully done—for you should have stepped back a pace as I fell for my foot in battle would have come up and knackered you and brought you down to handy throat-cutting distance. Now hand me up—though never give a Heathen that charity."

From then whenever he was free from his Atheling's duties, Justus began to turn warrior and make lasting friendship with Paternus.

*   *   *   *

So, the famine- and plague-struck year of 869 wore itself away with the Heathen Army at York. But in the tag end of that year it suddenly turned south and marched through Mercia into the lands of King Edmund of the East Anglians, and there was no standing against the Heathens. King Edmund was barbarously tortured and killed and his battle fyrds scattered and the Heathens became masters of all his lands.

The account of all this disaster came to the two brothers, King Ethelred and the Atheling Alfred on the same day that news came, too, that the good Archbishop Ceolnoth had died at Canterbury. A few days later, coming back from the Minster at Winchester after a service held in honour of the good Ceolnoth, the two brothers sat together in the King's chamber, both gloomy of face, each knowing the other's thought, and neither able to find any glimmer of good cheer to break the gloom which held them.

Suddenly Ethelred gave a sardonic laugh, and said, "Well, brother—now nears the time, and shortly, too, when in good earnest comes the turn of the West Saxons. There is no escaping the Heathen swarming."

"Nor should there be, my brother. We have done what we could. We are as ready as we can be. The fyrds stand waiting their call and as the Danes march then every man in their path must be swift to join the death-stand. We should send our wives and children west to Somerset ... Aye, beyond reach and beyond thought."

"They will travel hard for women. Godgifu is with child again. Pray this time she does not miscarry." He grinned. "You have been blessed in your choice of mare that she gives you so soon another child—and that a boy."

"Children we must have—and sons at that to keep the line of the House of Cerdic running."

"Though perhaps without a kingdom to inherit ..."

"You let your mind darken too readily, brother. God, for good but not always understandable reasons, gives the ones who hold his faith many trials and defeats to make them show that they hold boldly to His worship. There must be the seasons of good and bad. Winter frost breaks the iron hard plough furrows to good tilth and cropping."

"Always you have an answer."

"And a comforting one, I hope. We have done our work to

make this kingdom ready. Me by hard riding to ready our aldermen and thanes with their fyrd levies and you ..."

"You hesitate? And me?"

"By being king, and known to be king and, not least, by the prayers you make which are longer and more heart-sprung than many a monk's or priest's. No man goes into battle without a prayer—but coming out safely the habit falls from his mind until the next time he faces the Heathen swarm." Alfred stood up and swung his cloak over his shoulders. "Now I go to make our women and their house-holds ready."

"See that they have good guard. This country swarms with hungry bands who hold no allegiance to ought but their bellies. They need strong escort to Glastonbury."

"Which shall be."

Leaving his brother Alfred went to his wife's quarters where he found her suckling their son. Elswitha smiled at him and said, "He has a thirst that would not shame a man-at-arms, my lord."

"'Tis good—for that one day is what he must be, though I pray that his times will show less trouble than ours. But for now, know this from the King, my brother. You and your women and the children will ride with Godgifu and her household west to Glastonbury. I would come with you, but have other work. I go to counsel Ethelwulf, the Alderman of Berkshire at Reading. When the Heathen come it will be, I think, by way of his lands."

"You ride this day?"

"It was in my mind. But seeing you—" he grinned slowly "—I have changed my fancy to another more pleasing. I leave at dawn tomorrow and with your kindness will ride warm from your bed."

"As my lord pleases."

Late that afternoon after an hour's hard work with sword and shield on the cobbles of the royal yard, the off-duty guards and men-at-arms watching them and shouting taunts and encouragement to first one then another, Paternus sweating like a pig and Justus no less so went to the guard room, stripped and washed themselves down and then, clad only in their trews, sat and shared together a great horn of ale.

"So now," said Paternus smiling, "you begin to feel your oats and show me fancy tricks you think will fool me—the double feint and the nicely timed but false stumbles to put me off guard. 'Tis good—but set not too much store by such. Good swordsman you are and will be better, but never—and this remember—will you ever be so skilled with the long blade as some men."

"You for one?"

"Aye, me. And many another I could name. And many another among the Heathen that no doubt the Devil named. Could you turn me into marshman? To walk a night path with no less sound than an otter or fox?"

"I doubt it. Your feet are the wrong feet for such—though I could teach you much."

"And so I teach you. But born gifted you are not. You are good, but among the Heathen there are those who have the sword and axe and scramaseax feel which comes from years of use . . . aye, so that their limbs and muscles do their thinking for them without bidding. So—when the time comes—and a Heathen rushes you, shouting and possessed with his fighting devil, keep colder than ice. 'Twill be hard, for the men with you will be some drunk to rouse their courage, some flaming from past memory of wife gutted and childrens' heads smashed against a tree trunk. Oh, yes, marshman, keep ice cold. Do that—and live if so be the Lord's will."

"You give great comfort."

"A fair return for you comfort me as a son. Though son I never had to see, though that is another and not soon to be told story. But now, I give you easier news. Tomorrow we ride with my party to escort the King's lady and also the Lady Elswitha with their children and household to the West. We ride easy there and hard back for your Atheling Alfred but lends your service and mine to the Lady Godgifu's household. Now tell me—you have found a woman here to warm you at night?"

Justus laughed. "Nay—but why?"

"But why? There's a plaguing cuckoo word. And the why of it is that young blood can only be denied so long and I would not have you roistering in the town stews."

"So?"

"I will be frank. I have a wife here and with us visits often her younger sister ... aye, a pretty piece and sad for her husband who had his own yardland at Wimborne took the black sickness a year ago and died. 'Twas no great marriage of love, but a sound and sensible one. She says nothing—but she is woman and—"

"And you would find her husband to bring the sun sparkle back into her eyes."

Paternus grunted deep in his throat—and then grinned. "I do not look so far ahead. But sometimes comfort comes not amiss between friends and friends' friends."

"So many friends you mouth. But I take you kindly. So now you are free when we come back from the West to ask me to sup one night. I would not throw a kindness back into any man's face."

"Then we say no more. Now, off with you and get your gear packed. For war gear I will see you set—and one day you will pay me for it, and let it not be far away for I know your Atheling is kind to you—and I am a poor desperate man who would kill for a silver shilling so—" As he finished speaking Paternus picked up his dagger from the bench beside him and thrust at Justus's throat before Justus could move. He sat there with the point just touching his gizzard.

Withdrawing the dagger Paternus roared with laughter and then said, "To see the whiteness of your face. So you might look down into the dead face of Heathen and find his dagger in your throat. No heathen body is a dead one until the blow flies swarm as you come to it."

"That I will remember."

"Do that—and live longer than some. Now get to your Atheling."

*   *   *   *

The next morning Justus rode out in the bodyguard to the royal ladies going West, and that evening when Arnulf came back from his work and had stripped and was washing himself from the cauldron of hot water which Riada had had waiting for him, he said, "So, the royal ladies have ridden West this day."

"Aye, as I marketed I watched them go up the hill to the North gate." Riada came to him, carrying his clean shirt and trews and his linen house tunic.

"Well, so too we shall soon ride for I am lent to Sherborne to the Abbot. With the work goes a lodge and garden that stands above the river Yeo. With the way things pass in this country now 'tis a safer place from the Heathens than here."

"Aye."

"And no long distance from our own people. So, come the good weather, you could go back to Athelney and show them our children. For old folk that is a kindness."

"Aye."

Arnulf looked at her sharply, his face changing, and said, "Something troubles you?"

"Nay ... aye, but yes. And I would it did not."

"Then tell me."

Riada looked directly at him and then, with the wetness of tears in her eyes, said, "From you I can hold nothing. But I would have you know that neither can anything change what is between us though—" she smiled a little through her tears, "—you must be kind with what is probably only a fancy."

"If I am ever less than kind then the Devil take me for his own. Now speak. There must only be truth between us."

"Then speak I do, since I could not hold this to myself alone—though, I swear you, if it is a truth it shall make—can never make—any difference between us. But as I watched the guard go by with the royal ladies there was a man who rode with the Master of Arms whose face I only saw but briefly. And it had the look and shape of Justus's face. Maybe it was a woman's fancy ... but you must not blame me for that, or for always being honest with you."

Arnulf, stopping from drawing on his linen house tunic, was severe of face for a while and then smiled. He went to her and put his arm around her and said gently, "I am far from blame. But miracle it must be if it were Justus. What would you have me do?"

"That must be with you."

"Aye, so. It would not be hard to find out. That you would wish?"

"Only one wish I have. I am your wife and nothing alters that. But if Justus lives, that matters, for it takes final comfort and healing to an old ache. I have thought of him dead for so long that he is dead for me. But there would be a kindness in knowing him alive and in good service and he, too, in the way of finding the kind of happiness which has come to me. I say no more. I have long done my mourning and found my happiness."

"You speak with only the truth and goodness which a woman can know. I shall find out. And so, if it is true, it is a God-touched turn which so soon takes us to Sherborne."

With tears in her eyes Riada put her arms around him and kissed him, saying, "You are a good man and I shall ever be good wife to you."

Two days later Arnulf returned from his work and said to Riada, "I have spoken to one of the monks who is free of the royal household for he goes from time to time to read from the Bishop's books to the Atheling Alfred who now begins to take an interest in such things and shows much understanding of them and he is also much befriended by the Atheling's wife's mother—the good lady Eadburgh who too feeds this same appetite in the young Atheling. And so I have learned that it was in truth Justus whom you saw."

Riada was silent for a while and then said faintly, "So be it. And glad for him I am that he lives. And glad, too, that we go to Sherborne."

"You would know the full story of Justus—for it is a strange and brave one?"

"No. It is enough that he lives. One day, perhaps, I will ask you for it. But I am content at the moment with knowing that he lives." She went to him then and put her arms around him and kissed him, and he held her close and with a never to be spoken understanding of her heart-stir and the love and loyalty she gave to him.

A week later they rode to Sherborne and there, as the year wore to mid-summer, with unspoken understanding and love for her he marked the slow return of their married peace which had been tried for a while but now flowed calmly along its old course.

*　　　*　　　*　　　*

That year, too, Justus killed his first man. Riding with the Atheling Alfred's small escort back from Chippenham—where the Atheling had had meeting with the local Alderman and had been rough and outspoken with near anger at the man's lack of preparation in the matter of his fyrd-men and of his openly out-spoken disbelief that the Heathen, now fat and content in East Anglia, would ever come West—they were night bound by bad weather and deeply mired downland ways. At first light, after hard, wet lying, they were attacked by a band of homeless, outlawed and plunder-hungry men.

They came out of the growing dawn light like a pack of wolves, some well-armed, some ragged and boasting only cudgels and daggers; hungry, ravenous men, outcasts and landless, and long lost to any loyalty but the overlordship of their too often empty bellies.

The Atheling's guard made firm circle and as Alfred met the charge with his men, Paternus flanked him left and Justus stood to his right and they took the charge which, even as it came through the dawn's growing light, faltered a little and spread wide as the homeless band saw that they had picked for prey no benighted party of travelling merchants or priests with their bishop. But hunger and the lust for loot drove them on.

A long-haired bearded man ran at Justus, axe raised, howling wolf-like, and Justus took the weight of the blow on his shield and with his sword thrust him through his guts. Drawing back his blade to face another man he saw for the first time the red run of blood on his weapon. Three men he killed and yet had time to mark the calmness with which Alfred and Paternus stood and took the onslaught and heard Paternus laugh loud and then shout derisively, "A party of nuns with their bodkins would be over-match for these dogs."

Alfred laughed, too, and shouted, "Aye—but a stout bodkin in the right place makes a neater job than a sword."

In a few minutes the attack was beaten off and the living outlaws ran, leaving their dead.

Paternus, coming to Justus and still laughing, said, "Make no notch on your tally stick for these dogs. They eat their own kind." Then putting a firm friendly hand on Justus's shoulder he said gently, "Even so—you tremble like a girl. Take no shame from it. So it is with all first killing. But after time you will think no more of it than a slaughter-man does of sticking a pig."

Alfred coming to them said, "Paternus—"

"My lord?"

"See these rascals buried."

Surprise filling his face Paternus said, "Buried, my lord?"

"Aye. Rascals they are. But they are God's children and our countrymen and I would they had this last charity for clearly they got little as they lived. Were they Heathens the crows and foxes could have them."

"Aye, my lord. It shall be done."

Two days later Justus took supper at Paternus's home, ate venison and drank strong ale, and met for the first time his wife—a round, beaming, homely body who cheerfully bullied her husband, and also his wife's sister, Helburga—a comely, fair-haired woman in her early thirties with blue cornflower eyes who held herself demurely but without shyness, and was in no way put out by the rough jokes of Paternus which seldom lacked a touch of bawdiness. Justus liked her, but knew that liking and friendship and, if it were to come about, a body-gifting were all that he had to give any woman if she should so wish.

Late that night, sword at his side, he walked her to her home just within the Southgate, a small cottage standing close to the river side where two mornings later as he lay with her he could hear the splash of fat trout rising to a hatch of flies.

Lying content and naked in his arms Helburga said, "You think I am loose woman ... aye, and maybe rough-mouthed Paternus my pander?"

Justus laughed. "I would be standing by when anyone called Paternus pander to his face for it would be the last word the caller would speak. No, I think you are good woman—aye, and beautiful—but you are as I am."

"Which is what?"

"Dead to love—but alive to the comforts of friendship and the needs which are part of a body's nature. But that said— since the times are what they are and men are always hungry for more than food and drink—I think you do unwisely to live here alone."

"Give me answer to that then."

"You have it already. I serve the Atheling but not as I once did for service that kept me at nights within his call. Now I am of his bodyguard with Paternus and sleep only at the palace on duty nights."

She smiled and gently raised his caressing hand and bit the edge of it firmly, then said, "And on such nights I sleep at Paternus's house—"

"And God pity the man who enters there without leave."

"So—there is no more need for words and in return I will serve you well, trim your beard and keep your clothes as befits your position. That pleases you?"

"Since I am pleased already before seeing you, then am I now double pleased."

"And if I have child?"

"Then it shall have proper churching and sworn father to carry it to christening."

So Justus and Helburga lived in her riverside lodge while the year wore itself away and the plague throughout the land passed and the hard-saved seed corn grew from green spike to full golden ear and the garth trees bowed their branches under the weight of their fruit and the vineyards on the slopes about Winchester turned heavy with grapes, and all Wessex hoped that the Heathen men would stay content with their gains in East Anglia. All, that is, except those men who knew that greed feeds on greed and that the strongest greed in man is for the land which lies over the near horizon. And even those who were warriors plain and simple among the Heathen Armies who thought themselves untouched by such craving began to find that the season of their early lust for war had its changes ... the lust remained but was new shaped ... land they wanted, but the land over the horizon for surely that must be richer and crop heavier than the land they had gained ...

"Always," said Alfred talking with his brother the king, "it is an offence to the eyes to see a neighbour's field crop heavier than your own. Always the land beyond the horizon is a paradise to be reached. I tell you the Heathens will not be content with their gains. They will come—for the push from the bottom of the heap of their ant-hill will in the end make it topple. After so many seasons a warrior seeks comfort and a safe place to hang his sword and armour, but the sons of those warriors will not settle while there is another and more enticing paradise awaiting them. Wessex now stands alone—for Wales offers them nought but mountains and deer —and Mercia has gone, Northumbria too. As God reigns in heaven, brother, our turn comes. And when they come it will be with a swiftness to surprise all for though their dragon ships lie idle in the Eastern estuary and rivers, the word passes that now they take themselves to horseback—though I am told they ride like bears on a barrel."

"You paint a dark picture ..." Ethelred broke off into a fit of coughing, holding his hands to his shaking chest.

When the spasm had passed Alfred said, "So I do. For bright pictures and fancies are for the monks as they illuminate their parchments. I would have your leave to call the fyrds now and go to the Thames at Reading and pass the winter there for as God dwells in heaven that way they must come but knowing us there will perhaps be stayed from giving battle."

King Ethelred shook his head angrily. "You ask too much. Not of me but of my people. For the Mercy of God ... we have had a famine year and the crops are yet not fully gathered, and the talk grows hard against us in the country."

"Think you that I talk of demons and slaughter which are merely nightmares in my mind?"

"Enough!" The word was curt and brutal.

Alfred's face tightened. Then in a quiet voice he said, "Yes, my lord and king."

But back in his own quarters in the Palace Alfred sent for Paternus—for what he had in mind was something not to be trusted to anyone near the king.

When Paternus came Alfred was still curt from anger. He held out a heavy gold arm ring on which was chased a running pattern of beasts and birds and was bossed with a medallion incised with the letter A in flowing lines. He said sharply, "Take this and tell me is there any carl, yeoman or thane from here to Reading who would not know its owner?"

Scarcely bothering to look at it for he knew it well, Paternus, said, "No, my lord."

"Then mark this. You ride from here to Reading to the Alderman of Berkshire. On the way you give these, my words, to every man of proper standing in all towns and villages, and finally to the good Alderman Ethelwulf himself. On the first sign of any move of the Heathen Army west-wards to the Alderman's country some high beacon fire is to be lit, and so the same in every village and steading which has good vantage point to give warning back here—and, to follow that from Reading to here, good horsemen to carry the news and pass it on to his next horsed neighbour."

"Yes, my lord. And do I ride alone?"

"No, take one with you—Justus, for he is a man of sense and courage should aught happen to you and can carry out your part. And Paternus—this thing rests between me and you and Justus. I would not have my brother, the king, troubled, for he is a sick-growing man and I take upon my shoulders some of his labours—though secretly since I would not offend him."

"Have no fear, my lord."

*   *   *   *

Oricson, coming from guard duty into the lodgings which he had in Thetford—for now, being raised to guardmaster to Sidroc the Elder who was chieftain under King Bagsac who commanded the Heathen Army, he had to have quarters close to the king's residence—surprised Ina vomiting into a wooden bowl.

Concerned, he said anxiously, "What ails you, woman?"

Ina straightened, wiped her mouth with the hem of her gown, and smiled. "Naught—'tis but a belly heave from the fish we ate. I thought at the time—"

He stepped forward and took her arm roughly, saying, "Give me the truth, woman. I, too, ate of the fish but my belly is sound."

"Then it is stronger than mine."

"You think I am so easily fooled? You carry."

"I do not."

"Swear it."

"On what?"

"Swear it on your love for me."

"I swear on my love for you that I am not with child. It is truth—I did but eat bad fish. Are you disappointed?"

"I know only this—that it would give me happiness to have child by you. Though the gods know the times are not right for it since as soon as the New Year is well in the Army marches."

"That pleases you. And it pleases me for I shall be with it in the baggage train. I swear to you it was but fish—but I would have your child since you have been good to me and given me place where I had none before. And where marches the Army?"

"You are fool that you cannot guess? Westwards and southwards to the fat lands—though they stand less fat than

130

they should since the year has been bad for them—though in that good for us since their men will have less heart to answer the death-stand call. Here, too, many come from oversea, crowding after us and settling. Aye, and so would I do if I had more years to my tally ... Aye, and so will I do with you after a few more years. Now clear away that bowl and find me food and when it darkens we will lie abed and I will tell you the story of how Sigurd gained the gift of being able to understand the language of the singing birds."

"Who was Sigurd?"

He laughed and then almost shouted, "You ask me that when I have told you a hundred times before? Ah, yes, to tease me into the play you love. Come here—" he took her in his hands, swung her round and over his thigh and, hoisting her gown, began to slap her bare behind while she wriggled and choked with laughter to balance his.

5

Two days after Candlemas in the year 871, on a night of iron hard frost and a sky so clear that the stars shone near and large, the warning beacon began to burn from Alderman Ethelwulf's town of Reading on the river Thames. Long before dawn the warning pyres flared across the land, as Alfred the Atheling had planned, and gave the signal to the winter fyrds that were barracked about Winchester. At first light King Ethelred's army rode out and the town people gathered to see them go. In the crowd stood Paternus's wife and her sister, Helburga. As the Atheling's men rode by both Paternus and Justus raised hands and smiled cheerfully at them and then were gone.

Paternus's wife turned away with Helburga and sighed, saying, "They go with an eagerness no woman can understand. They raise their hands and smile and then out of sight so are we forgotten."

"They go for our sakes."

"Aye—and be not deceived—for the sake of this good land of Wessex. But they go also because they love the slaughter. They will pray for peace in the land before the minster altar. But granted peace they would soon find life as dull as ditchwater."

"I think not."

"Then you are addle-pated."

Helburga smiled, but made no reply. In her mind though were the memories of many talkings she had listened to lying in bed with Justus and among them some words which she could never forget—*The good Lord, our God, put man into Eden, and man was cast from it by his own lust. Maybe that was*

God's design—that he would lose Paradise but then through untold years should blindly seek and finally find an earthly Paradise of his own making.

If Justus, riding on the left hand of Alfred, could have been reminded of those words at that moment he would have given them small heed. Now, for the first time, he was riding, armed and in a great company to meet the Heathen men at last, the men who had taken him from Riada, men whom he had seen pillage, rape and plunder his own people, and men who had taken him into captivity. Pray God, he thought, that the lines of destiny ran true and one day he should meet Oricson in battle with the Heathen Host.

Three days later King Ethelred's army was met west of Reading in the land between the rivers Kennet and Thames by Alderman Ethelwulf. They sat in King Ethelred's battle tent and the stocky, broad-shouldered Alderman, his brown, wrinkled face beaming above his beard, gave them good and bad news.

"Two days ago, my lord King, we met the Heathen host that came from Reading. There they hold the town and already throw up defences across the land between the Kennet and Thames rivers. I do not say it was full host we met, but of a number the like of which I have not seen before. But we held the shield wall, my lord, and then drove them back. Few words to describe great doings. Two of their great leaders were slain, but as yet I can give them no name. We held the death-stead—but full glad I am to see you for they will spare little time to lick their wounds before they come again."

Alfred, passing a tankard of wine to the stout Alderman, said, "They come to stay—or to plunder and pass? Speak frankly."

The Alderman shrugged his shoulders. "To stay if we let them. To plunder and pass if not. But one truth holds—they are sworn to stay in Wessex until they have picked its bones. Mercia, Northumbria, East Anglia—now comes our turn unless ..."

"Unless what?" asked King Ethelred testily.

"Unless we are men enough to stand to them and hammer them in a way which no others have. And though I am

Mercian myself I take shame for my countrymen there—drive me out though they did. Here I am Wessex man and swear that no raven-winged Heathen shall rest in my lands while I live and can swing sword or battle axe."

King Ethelred coughed and beat his chest for ease and then said, "To that Amen. And pray the good Lord to stand on our side. Now, you will do me favour. Take my brother with you and ride with him the country around so that he marks the lie of the land and all such other knowledge that he should know. And, my brother, as you go, pray send my priest to me—for if tomorrow is a time of battle, then today is a time for prayer."

Outside the tent the Alderman as he walked to his horse glanced aside at Alfred and, reading the look on his face, said, "Without discourtesy, my Atheling, and in no way shouldering aside the power of prayer, I fancy that these are times and this the place when He would forgive us a little shortening of holy ritual."

Alfred grinned. "I am sorry, good Ethelwulf, but from long riding and lack of sleep my ears are full waxed and I lose your words. But if it were a share of your battle plunder you were offering, I accept the gift."

The Alderman bellowed with laughter and slapping his thigh said, "You shall take your pick."

*   *   *   *

The next morning, long before first cock-call, Justus was in attendance on his Atheling. The priests had given all the Saxon warriors their Mass prayers and all men stood ready for the coming day. Ahead of them the Heathen host, withdrawn to high ground, stoutly palisaded with stakes and heavy timbers, waited before Reading for the Wessex men to march.

Deftly Justus serviced his master in his dressing. Alfred—silent and with the look on his face which forbade speech unless he gave it first—was quickly accoutred. He wore a plain round helmet of Baltic steel, though all the Army rank and file were happy if they could claim helmets of soft Wealden iron instead of thick, hardened leather ones. In silence he was dressed and there was no stir of his bearded face until with a sudden swift smile, he said, "Go, Justus, and make good your own wants, and pray God to carry us through this day." As Justus left he saw his master drop slowly to one knee in the act of prayer. Mass in public was for the heartening of all, but after that each man found time to make his own prayer, even though he did it as he belted on his gear or chewed the hard comfort of near frozen bacon and bread hunk; for the morning was of flesh- and finger-numbing coldness and the ground rang like a drumskin with the passage of men and horses.

Coming to Paternus, long abroad and ready and beaming like a boy who knows that it is fairing day and full of promising pleasures, the warrior said, "You have eased your bowels this morning? Good. Then remember this: we stand on either side of the Atheling—he is as raw in battle as you are. So take heart. More I will not say for I know there is little that words can do. And should I call for turning and running know that it comes from good sense, not cowardice. He who turns away—lives but to fight another day. But first, think too of what these Heathens have done to our peoples ... aye, and to you."

Justus, stirred, said sharply, "I am for killing and should my turn come—then so be it."

"Nicely said. But save it for when the horn cups are raised for victory and the mead runs."

So, Justus went into battle, and the Saxon men and the Berkshire fyrds stormed the rising ground to the palisaded defences which the Heathens had raised up before Reading ... Heathen men now seen for the first time in battle, carrying double-handed axes and broad swords, and others with throwing javelins and arrowed bows. And all that morning under the weak winter sun the Danes stood firm, the palisade unbreached. On both sides men died, some to go screaming or cursing to their death, some suddenly to halt in their stride as arrow took their throat and they dropped with a

135

last blood-choked whimper as of a child in pained sleep.

When, at last, the palisade was breached the Heathen came out and met them on the ground and Justus took his first kill as a winged-helmeted savage leaped for him, great axe swung aloft. As it fell, Justus side-stepped and scythed him sideways with his sword and near severed his head from his body, and Paternus roared, "Neatly done—Valhalla give him welcome!" Between them, sweating and bloodied now with his own first killings, the Atheling Alfred laughed grimly, but said nothing for he was beyond words. He could see now that this day could never be theirs since they had breached the palisade only to loose a tide of warriors who now swarmed down to them in a raging sea.

Long they held them, but in the end King Ethelred gave the word to fall back which they did in good enough order while the Heathens, hard-reined from the lust to follow by their chieftains, halted and jeered them over the skyline.

That night the Saxon host made camp two miles to the westwards on the high slopes of a long chalk ridge of the downs, and there King Ethelred and his brother Alfred heard the news for the first time that the good Alderman Ethelwulf had been killed in a last charge on the Heathens before they had turned from their pursuit in an unmarshalled victory-chanting mob to their palisaded hill camp.

Sitting in their shared war tent, campaign table set, cold meat and wine before them, King Ethelred, coughing as the ice-cold air touched his throat, said dispiritedly, "He was good man—though a Mercian."

Sharply Alfred answered, "You forget, my brother King, that my wife and your lady are Mercians. These are days now when every man in this land not a Heathen is countryman."

Ethelred grunted. "Aye, so I do—and take back my words." He sighed. "Well ... what is there to be done? They will have Reading and we must find the war-geld to pay them to go."

Roused, Alfred said, "My lord, my brother—all know that is no way to treat with them. They will go but to return. This is now but their winter sport. They would go—and next year be back, and the year after and—"

Ethelred shook his head and said, "You do not see my reasoning. All you say is true—but you look not far enough ahead. Since we are here we will give them battle ... aye, may take victory in these following days. Let that be, and let Wessex men see what shape the years ahead have—and those days will be yours for mine I know, by God's will, are to be short in number and you will be king. You have the strength and the years that God now denies me ..." He laughed grimly. "You see it not yet—but I seek to buy you time to shape this land and our people to chase the Heathen from our lands for ever."

"You are beyond me, brother."

"Then have trust in my words. So we will make good show for them, take one day's victory with another's defeat and in the end settle for this time with a hard bargained ransom. You do not move with my thinking?"

"It is hard to take—but I see now some wisdom in it."

"Then keep it to yourself."

And so it was that in the following hard days the Heathens came out from Reading and fought the Saxons and were put to rout, losing many of their great warrior chiefs. But still Reading stood in their hands. Then, nearing the coming of Lent, the two hosts fought again and this time the victory went to the Heathens. So, like a tide coming and going without settled rhythm for ebb and flow, victory and defeat marked each side. Finally, the Heathen chiefs offered peace at the price of heavy Saxon ransom which was paid. The Danish army marched eastwards from the country of the West Saxons as the battle winter passed into Spring and each fyrd man thought now more of seeding-time than sword-time, and Alfred who had become king on the death of his brother, King Ethelred, who was buried at Wimborne, found himself alone with a near broken army and a West Saxon land unploughed and unseeded and with no direction in his mind of the way he should turn and work to build a shield for his land against the Heathens and the certainty of their return.

As the Heathen Army took its way east and made camp for the night on the banks of the lower Thames, Oricson, lying under the stars close to Ina, the two wrapped in furs and cloaks, said, "I have not spoken this before, but three times in the last long weeks in going against the Saxons I have seen a man fighting in the Saxon royal guard who had much the look of Justus."

"Could your eyes deceive you?"

"Aye, easily in battle for one gives scant time to a man's face. 'Tis his sword or spear arm you watch."

"But you called him marshman. None such would be fitted for a royal guard."

Oricson laughed and pulled her close to give and take body warmth. "You know not Justus. He built a boat, 'tis said, the like of which had not been seen before and then he sailed it and gave command to the sea and wind to take him safely back to this country. Even had the ship foundered under him in gale, then some sea monster would have risen kindly from the deeps and horse-backed him to shore. Aye ... long believing it is—but I am sure it was Justus. Just once I crossed swords with him shortly when we battled at Wilton and for a marshman he handled his blade well."

She laughed. "Pity 'tis that he had not known you for he might have given you his promised words and your score could have been settled. What words I wonder would have passed?"

"I know not nor care not since I know they would be the last he should speak." He was silent for a while, and then with a sigh said, "'Tis good land the Saxons have—aye, and cattle and horses, though their crops will be thin this year. But one day we shall take our pick of such ... no pinching strip of yardland, but a handful of hidelands, watered and wooded and pastured. And you will put your mind to it and take no marsh trick herbs to stop it—and give me children."

"And if I do not?"

"I will sell you to a Frankish merchant for slave and find myself another."

*　　*　　*　　*

138

Sitting in the early summer sun in Helburga's garden, Justus, free from royal guard duty for two days, watched the marbled flow of the waters, the spreading weed growths waving gently in the current like the long green tresses of mermaiden and the belly flash of trout and grayling as they took fly nymphs and water snail. Contentment moved in him to run with the sharp throat-touch of the wine he drank. Helburga, sitting on the grass beside him, looked up, smiled at him and said, "You are long silent. Yet I think there is something in your mind ... almost I can hear it buzzing like a bee. What is it?"

"It shows?"

"Aye—now and again like the quick turn of a fish underwater. Though whether it is from sorrow or happiness I cannot guess."

"Then neither—for I have had the first and now possess the second."

"For a marshman you turn words nicely."

"There's no strangeness there. My people understand the talk of birds and take some music from them. And a good marshman can finger a lyre and sing as good a skald as any Heathen ... though of a gentler nature."

"So tell me what is it that now and then clouds your face."

Justus sighed, and then with a shrug of his shoulders said, "So I do. I think King Alfred intends some new service for me. He has said little but I can guess more—and it could take me away for long from here."

"As king's guard?"

"No—sadly."

"Then what?"

"Leave the *what* to wing a while. I would know whether you would marry me and come with me. I shall have good escort—for the journeying would be long."

"We have no need to marry. You must know by now that I cannot bear child."

"Only God knows that, and—" he grinned, "—a good prayer might turn the trick. But I would know your answer, though I cannot now give you the reasoning for my journeys since it is not fully known to me."

"Then without answer from you—I will give you answer. Yes, I will go with you."

"For that answer my heart gives thanks. But married we must be. I would have no one name you wrong or point the finger at you."

Helburga laughed, and said mockingly, "Aye, my lord, if it pleases you."

Justus stood up, reached for her and brought her into his arms and kissed her. Letting her go, he said, "I leave you now for it is set that I talk with the king at noon and he is sharp with any man who keeps bad time."

"You like him?"

"I honour him, and am sad for him since there is a loneliness in him which I have tasted myself at times. But he is not a man one likes in the ordinary way of men. He stands alone and his loneliness is like a dark cloud around him."

"You have gained a smooth tongue over the years. Honey me with it to bed when you come back."

Shortly after noon, Justus was given an audience by King Alfred. He was sitting in his chamber off the great reception hall of the palace, the sun coming through one of the narrow, deeply recessed windows to fall across a lectern at which sat a monk who had been reading to him from one of the brightly illuminated manuscripts which belonged to the bishop. Alfred raised a hand to stay the monk in his reading. For a moment or two, plain-faced, he studied Justus, and then slowly smiled. He liked and respected this man who had served him well, but, more than that, he had the slowly growing conviction that in some way their destinies were linked—though not in battle work against the Heathens. There were others who would serve him in that and for years to come. Justus was good warrior, but could never be as Paternus and others.

Abruptly, he said, "You spoke to me once about your days with the Heathens and your work as a shipwright, and the making of your small escape boat—and beyond that the need an island kingdom must always have for a war fleet to protect its shores ..."

"I did, my lord."

"Words I took to heart. And which—since I am now king —mean to bring to life." He paused and smiled. "Your mind runs with me?"

"I have heard talk, my lord, that it is your wish to have ships built ... a fleet to meet the Heathen boats at sea."

"Then you have heard true. It will be a long business ... years. But it must be done ... must be begun in my time. Already the word has been passed—but I need someone to go in turn to all our shipwrights and make plain to them the kind of war-craft we need. Of this I know little—but you shall supply my default there. You will find them a stubborn lot. Handle them gently, but get your way. Though, if you get your way fully, I shall be surprised. Keeping full control of an army in battle is beyond the greatest leader. Turning a craftsman from his set ways the same. But you will use my written authority, your presence, and your knowledge to gentle them into the shaping of the craft we need. You will have protection on your journeyings—and carry my royal warrant. So what think you?"

Justus smiled. "I am young, my lord. I shall talk to men twice or more my age. But with God's good grace, my lord, you shall have your war craft."

"Aye, so I shall—but I doubt whether I shall get the full form of the ships which live in your mind's eye. Time and experience are the twin masters of true change—and men have little enough of the first and are often slow to learn from the second. But go—and serve me, not now with a sword but with your dream which has also become mine."

That evening Justus and Helburga ate with Paternus and his wife, and Paternus, a little drunk, was full of advice.

"I have picked you two men to ride with you. But, when you can, join some party of merchants or priests who journey your way, and take an open road whenever you can. To see ahead is the first part of safety. Woods are for villains—in which this island favours them for it is more forest than aught else. Now show me that warrant again—for God knows I have never had brother-in-law nor any close kin that ever carried such."

As Justus laughed and handed him the rolled parchment Paternus's wife said, "Married they are not yet."

"We go to the priest tomorrow," said Helburga.

"And spend your wedding night in some ale-house on the way to Swanage? Hard lying for such a night," said her sister.

" 'Tis no matter—that night was spent long ago."

"Aye," roared Paternus, "—then that follows pattern for there are more marriages consummated before consecration in this country than there are sand grains on the seashore. And in that matter my dear wife and I stand—"

"Paternus—enough!" ordered his wife sharply.

"Enough! Always the woman's cry. Well ... well ... I will be proper as a priest." He raised his tankard and, with a little bow to Justus and Helburga, said kindly, "God be good to you both and give you a full quiver and warm lying on cold nights."

The next day Justus and Helburga, stoutly mounted on two sturdy cobs and with a pack horse for their gear, rode out after their marriage on to the road to Swanage with a party of monks and tradesmen. As they rode Helburga said to Justus, "You have made good woman of me—and I will be good wife to you. That is our goodness—but the months ahead, I fear, will be hard for you. You go to men who are set in their ways and seek no change. Your temper can be quick."

"Aye, I know. But already I begin to school myself to patience. Rome was not built in a day ... aye, now, there's a place I would like to see ..."

*   *   *   *

Towards the end of the following year, 872, Noth saw launched down the slipway a dragon ship which he had built for Oric's lord at Hedeby and which Oric was to man, armour and provision to join the great fleet of King Guthrum.

As they sat talking after the drinking and merry-making to mark the taking of its keel to the water for the first time, Oric said, "It is a fine craft. My lord will be pleased. Guthrum calls for a grand fleet for in a few years the word runs that things pass to a great change."

"Aye, I know. When the Saxon pickings grow few and lean and men have had years of pirating and easy plunder—then it is the good earth of the ravaged land they seek to hold."

"And with reason. Here, the land groans and grows miserly in crops under the many mouths to feed. Guthrum seeks to do now that which the Saxons once did—take that which cannot be carried away. The land itself. Not this year, nor next year but in a few years it will begin and only one kingdom now truly stands against its coming ... the Wessex lands held by the heirs of the Great Cerdic. And to tease you, and perhaps please you—I tell you that their new King Alfred has eyes that look more to the future than most men's. He sees what must come and prepares for it—for he, and only he, stands between the wish and the taking. He, too, begins to build a fleet to meet Guthrum's."

" 'Tis common-sense. But in what am I teased?"

"A twist of fate that links you with all this. The marshland Justus to whom you gave your crafts here has risen high in his homeland and now carries his king's warrant to watch over and control this ship-building."

Noth straightened his bowed back with a jerk and his old eyes grew bright as he said, "You have this for truth? I had long counted him dead for that was the only common-sense end to his mad fever."

"He lives. There are those at the Saxon court who bow their knees to Alfred—but with one hand behind their backs to catch the gold which Guthrum drops. Your marshboy, now man, made landfall though his butterfly boat was wrecked, and now serves his king in the shaping of the new Saxon craft."

"Then I give praise for that. That he lives."

"That I understand—but will keep close to myself. But there 'tis. His story is known widely in his land. Aye ...

and no doubt their Christian priests will make much of it in the writings of their annals."

"And so should they."

"You think that he will turn all the Saxon shipwrights and masters to his way of thinking—that they will have finer craft than ours?"

Noth laughed. " 'Tis not easy to teach old dogs new tricks. Some, maybe—but many not. Not even if in their hearts they see the good reasoning in a new trick. But for all that I have little thought. Only that he lives is enough for me. And Oricson—what news of him?"

"Little—he moves with the Army. But I have heard that like so many of his kind over there—the place begins to touch him. The fat lands and the good cattle. Were I young man now I would go. These words between us I would have you keep to yourself. It would do us no favour for it to be known that you schooled the marshman."

"They are safe with me."

For a moment or two Oric's face was severe with thought, and then he said, "I give you one leave should you wish to take it. And should you think it wise—"

"I read your mind. Gerda?"

"Yes."

"I shall tell her nothing. She has his son. For her Justus is gone and dead. There was only kindness and a seeking of comfort between them. Now she has her son—and one day he will be here in my place."

Long after Oric had gone, Noth sat watching the new dragon ship riding at anchor on the river, waiting now only for her final rigging and fitting out and, as the tide ran in and the wind scuffed the wave tops to blown spume, he remembered the day he had seen Justus come riding back on the wind-driven tide in his boat, and then he slowly smiled and said aloud, "Justus, Justus—now you have your own kind to deal with and being men there will be more closed than open minds among them. Then comes the time when you will need a silver tongue and will find that with some it will not be enough to charm them from their old ways. They will

144

kiss your hand and the king's warrant and then when your back is turned go their old ways ..."

*   *   *   *

Which was true. Riding back from the yards down river from Exeter late one autumn evening where Justus had been in counsel with the master shipwright, his face was for a long time tight with anger at the thought of his past and fourth meeting with the man. Like so many of the others he had now met from Hampton westwards the man took his warrant from the king as simply an earnest of future payment for his yardmen's work ... *And good master Justus, you shall have such ships as my lord, the good King Alfred has never seen before ... of a size and strength and* ... Beyond that the man had no thought of considering seriously the size and shape and meetness to its coming purpose that must inform the design of the craft.

"All they look to," he complained bitterly to Helburga as they ate supper in their lodgings—late-run Exe salmon and a wortleberry pudding with thick cream to take the edge from its tartness, "is to build something bigger than heretofore—to carry more men—and with no thought to shaping it for handling in sea-fight. We shall end with a fleet of barges and the dragon ships will sail rings around us. Few of them see that you cannot bring the dragon ships to battle unless you can outsail and overhaul them and then lie abreast a few lengths and pick them off with ready bowmen. They wear no armour when they sail—and they are poor bowmen at best. We must have fast ships to come in and give them the death sting and ..." He stopped talking suddenly and looking up from his platter grinned. "Aye, you smile. And glad I am of it—for it brightens the end of the day." He took her hand and kissed it leaving the purple mark of his fruit-stained lips on it, and went on, "See, one would think I bruised your fair hand with my lips. I wish I could so easily bruise some minds into my way of thinking. More, too, this man down river looked askance at my royal letter—aye, and he not the

145

first—and, as joke with under-meaning, hinted that I might be some rogue come to cull him into all this work and then leave to collect Dane-geld from my true masters who would have us have a fleet to raise their laughter and mockery. I tell you, it is in my mind to go find the king and tell him all this. Some openly near-defy my warrant. What is a scrap of parchment with a scrawl some out-cast priest could have penned for beer money for himself and his doxy, and me a rascal working for Heathen gold?"

"Are there not some of your way of thinking, and honest men, too?"

"Aye ... a few. But when they turn to their wrights and labourers they find them mules that baulk from following a strange path without constant goading, and so time wears away. Oh, if only I could find a few Noths amongst them all."

"Ah, yes—your heathen god Noth."

"No heathen at heart. And now I tell you. Soon we ride with some merchants west to Plymouth and if any there question my warrant—then I ride to the King and risk his anger because my work goes poorly for want of true and not to be questioned gage of my standing. Parchment! Aye, that stands good for one who is of good faith and can read and then argues fairly against me, of which there have been a few. But for the others I need stronger sign."

Two days later as Justus walked in the morning from their lodgings to the stable to take his horse to ride down river to the yards, he turned from the street's end out on to the river-side quay and found himself face to face with Arnulf, who was carrying his plaited straw working basket over his shoulder. Both men stopped, each for a moment or two aware of waking memory and then searching for its true shape. It was Arnulf who spoke first.

He held out a hand, and said, "Good Justus. I had heard you were alive and back in this land. God give thanks for that."

"And I give you my thanks for a kind welcome. What do you here?"

"I stay but a few days longer. The monks give me work on

the fortress chapel roof. You, I hear, are close to the king and a man of importance."

"If that is what they say—let it ride. I do no more, perhaps less than you, than seek to repair and shape wooden walls. And since we are so met by chance and I would have nothing between us for I know you to be good man and the past is far distant, I tell you that I am happily married."

"As am I. Riada travels not with me. She stays at Wimborne with the two children—who both carry my name."

"So much I have long known. And since it was the way God willed it—I thank you for your goodness. And make also this promise to you—my child is yours. In no way shall my shadow fall across your threshold floor. Time eases all sorrows."

"Those are good words. You would I should tell Riada of this meeting?"

Justus laughed gently. "Why not? To hold silence over this would not fit your nature—nor mine. And Riada should she ever know you had would find it no kindness. The good Lord designs our ways—we should always walk them openly. So we part—but I would ask you one thing before going."

"Ask."

"I would know the name of the child so that it be remembered in my prayers."

"The boy's name is Otta since that was Riada's wish."

"It is a good name—and one I shall remember in my prayers."

A week later Justus was in Plymouth and found the people —who were largely of British and Celtic stock, though the whole lands of Devon and Cornwall acknowledged the sovereignty of the House of Cerdic—more stubborn than most. The Heathen threat was far from them and for the building of craft other than trading ships to pass between them and Brittany and fishing boats to take the rich catches from their waters they had no interest. But they were a well-spoken, easy mannered race who said *Yea* and *Nay* as they guessed would please Justus, but in their hearts had no intention of altering their manner of ship-wrighting to please a young man who had little more than half the years of the most of them. And this—although he liked them and they held back no courtesy from him—was all too clear to Justus. He needed more than a roll of parchment to impress them.

A month later King Alfred gave audience to Justus again in the same chamber at Winchester, and on a same sunny morning, and, indeed, with such a sameness about things that travel-worn and frustrated Justus had the wild thought that he had never been away. The monk who had been there before was reading aloud from a wide-leaved parchment manuscript so that Alfred could follow the words and take their understanding line by line.

The king heard him in silence through his reports and when he had finished, he said, "So you find the handling of men set in their ways a sore trial and would have something to stir them out of their old ways of thought?"

"I do, my lord."

The king shrugged his shoulders. "A while ago I would have had no patience with you and dismissed you and found another for my work. But now I know more wisdom—for the same stubbornness meets me with many an alderman and thane. Words and parchments set with demands are first soon forgotten and second thrust out of sight in a bedroom chest— and so life and labour stay in the same well-run path. And all this while the Heathen work and plan and one day will return. So—though my first mind was to dismiss you and find some other—I find charity and new understanding. You shall have three of my bodyguard to carry the Wessex Standard. And you shall carry me with you wherever you go."

"How so, my lord?"

King Alfred picked up from the open manuscript at his side the pointer with which he had been following the words as the monk read aloud to him. Handing it to Justus he said, "Take this and make known that it stands in my place and through you speaks for me. If any hastily deny it and with words oppose me—then let your bodyguard serve them as though they were warriors who from cowardice turned their

148

backs on the country's enemies in battle and ran for the saving of their own hides."

Looking down at the reading stick in his hand Justus saw that the tapered pointer, a hand's breadth in length, was of some hard, dark, finely polished foreign wood. At its head, shaped to fit the palm of the hand, was a pear-shaped jewel set in a gold mount, carrying a design of the figure of King Alfred, crowned, with his hands resting on a stool's arms, and wearing a short-sleeved tunic with a belt. He held in his hands two long-stemmed flowers that rested one over each shoulder. The bright enamels flashed in the sun from the window—white for the flesh, gold for the hair, green for the tunic and sky blue for the background, and the whole was covered with a plate of rock crystal set in a band of gold filigree round which ran the inscription—*Alfred ordered me to be made*. At its bottom was the golden head of a boar into whose mouth the butt of the stick pointer was set.

For a moment, bewildered by the mere possession of such a treasure, Justus was too over-awed to find words. Then, gulping to clear his throat, he said, "My lord King—this is too precious for my poor trust."

"Aye, may be. But you have it. And having it you have my presence with you wherever you go. If any man deny it—then he denies me. But remember this—these are poor times and men are hard-pressed. Be gentle and reason when you can. At others be hard, but never roughly force a craftsman to new skills or forms. Gentle him ... aye, and flatter him until he comes to the thought that all you ask has already been long in his mind. And do not forget, Justus, that since Rome was not built in a day—then neither will be your dream and mine of battle fleets to secure this land of ours. Make true for me the beginning of that dream. Now go and leave me to my word-reading for which in future I shall use some apple twig that, had I left it on its tree, would have shown in its time a flowering and beauty far outshining any jeweller's work. For God is the master of all craftsmen."

*   *   *   *

149

Towards the end of the year 872 Arnulf returned from Exeter to Sherborne to work on repairs to the minster roofing. Working aloft there on fine days with his men his eyes were delighted by the great stretch of country under his view ... forested hills, narrow river and brook valleys and the town spread below him so that the people walked like dwarfs under the shadow of the minster. Over the weeks as he worked with his men the pigeons which nested in the window embrasures and on the ledges and cornices of the building would come to them when they took their midday dinner hour and squabble and bully over the scraps of bread and cheese rind which were tossed to them. Arnulf delighted in the birds and felt in a far-fetched way that he shared part of their world, able to look down with them at the towns-folk, dwarfed and shrunken, as they went about their business.

There it was, on a golden noontide, autumn colourings brightening on all the forest and corn sweeps of the yard-lands, that as the birds circled high over head after feeding, swinging together in great flighting arcs, Arnulf sat on a parapet edge and watched them. As he looked upwards a pair of peregrine falcons stooped on the flock of birds from their high waiting pitch and came down in a long dive on the birds which scattered in alarm at the peril from above. A boy's bowshot above the tower the leading bird struck at the flock and made its kill while the rest of the flock dropped and tumbled to the tower top to seek refuge; and some in their panic winged across the parapets, the wind hissing from their wings. One of the birds flew straight into Arnulf's face as he raised his hands to ward it off. The raising of his hands and the blow in the face from the pigeon knocked him back off balance from his parapet seat and he dropped to the ground far below.

When his fellow workmen reached him it was to find him lying broken and dead across a pile of fresh hewn masonry blocks. Later, when one of the monks came to his lodging in the town to give the sad news to Riada, she with the instant foresight of a woman read the news on his face before his words could mark in sorrow the dreadful truth. She took his comfort unheeding for it was weak balm for the blackness of her spirit. When he was gone she walked from the lodging, leaving the two children in charge of the servant girl, and still-faced went into the woods and sat on a bank and hid her face in her hands and prayed for the soul of the man who had taken her into comfort and then drawn from her the growth of a love for him that near-matched his for her. After a little while her tears came and her body shook with the passion of her loss.

They gave him high funeral and seven days of altar prayers, night and day, for he was beloved of all the monks and the priests.

Then, before winter set the ground hard, Riada gathered her children and household goods and rode with a passing company of merchants west to the Athelney marshes to her parents for comfort. Arnulf had left her with good provision for the rest of her life, but apart from the lasting joy she took in her children and her caring for them, she needed more to still the sharp return of memories. The thane's wife, for whom she had worked before, took her under charge as a companion and embroidery worker—though each night she returned to sleep with her parents, for it was not meet that a well-formed handsome woman should rest at the Hall unguarded at night. Kind though the thane and his lady were, it was no place for a woman to rest without husband or protector, for many of the thane's companions, no matter their standing, were too used when in their cups to reach without charity for that which raised the fire of lust in them.

So that winter the two boys began to grow into the ways of the marsh people. Even though young still there was much difference between them, shown in small ways. Otta was daring and fearless, tumbling after his grandfather and his dogs, while Edmund—named for the martyred king by Arnulf—was a quiet child who would sit and play with a polished beach pebble as though through his hands it worked some deep pleasure in him, and when his grandmother sang some old song he would grasp his tiny fists tightly as though to contain some great joy.

One day Riada's mother said to her, "If God is kind and gives them their time they will be good sons. Though, I speak frankly—the one will always look upwards to the heights where his father laboured, and the other straight before him to mark and prepare for the passing of the way he sees ahead ..."

And, too, her father, blunter in his manner, said, "You know, there is talk that Justus now stands high with the king— or would you I did not speak his name?"

"There is no near pain in it now. But I will spare you, my father, a waste of words for I can guess how they might run. Justus is already married—and to a good woman. Our paths have long separated. That was God's will. Let it rest there."

"Then some other man. I speak frankly because you are woman and young still and—" he grinned, "—not without a handsome dowry. There are many good yeomen with yard-lands to their name would take you gladly for yourself and triple gladly for your dowry. Outspoken I may sound, but I think first of your comfort as a woman. Find that and, with the grace of the saints, you may come to love again. I would not have my daughter turn homespun nun. You are full woman and that you cannot deny any more than a flower bud can hold back from blossoming under the summer sun."

Riada laughed. "You should make a round of lays on that for some minstrel to sing in the thane's great hall. But I take you kindly. I am content with my lot until God sends true sign that I should change it. So no more of such talk."

"Nor will there be. But all griefs have their turn. But in this country—though it seems quiet at the moment—there is nothing certain except that time passes and one should use it looking to the front for happiness without back glance over the shoulder to the past. And having said that I will say no more. Except—" he gave her a sudden, warm grin, "—to tell you that cold though the mere waters are, your Otta already begins to splash and thresh in the shallows as though he would make a truth of his name. Otter he will be ... aye and much more beside."

*   *   *   *

It was not until the late summer of 872 that Justus learned of the death of Arnulf. Most of his time from early spring had been spent in the eastern parts of Wessex on the coast, cajoling and bullying many an awkward shipwright. But now his authority ran harder and firmer for at the sight of the king's jewel there were few men who did not in their imagination see the shape and the quick anger of the real king behind it. Yet given that, there was still the hard crust of their traditional ways of thinking to be overcome and here, more often than not, the final end was a compromise and slowly Justus learned to temper his obstinacy and settle for some middle way. He realized, too, that the men who would man the ships were of the wrong sort.

In the rare times when he now had counsel with the king he always came at some point to his main complaint—that it was no good to take land warriors and put them on shipboard to fight. Just as the king had his fyrds of land warriors to call on—men who were long and hard-trained to school their war-lust and follow without question the orders of their thanes and war-band commanders and so to fight with fair discipline—so then should there be shipmen warriors who lived with their craft and their captains and who would flight fire brands and arrows and spears at command, and know the trick and the time of rightness to close with the enemy and hold him to him with grappling irons for the final assault. Always on their now rare meetings he came to that point, and always he got the same answer, sometimes touched with resignation and sometimes sparking with the heat of kingly frustration—for the Cerdic Alfred could see ahead as easily as Justus but his basket of Wessex problems was already overflowing.

"Good Justus—you ask too much too soon. A man may see the truth of a matter ahead of him. But the reaching of its wholeness lies in time. We must use what we have at hand to serve us, and pray God to stand at our side and give us the years to come slowly to some nearness of the shaping of such dreams. It is in my mind, though, that never do men ever come to the joy of finding true shaping."

But often when Justus had gone, Alfred would go on his knees and pray to God in His wisdom to shorten such waiting times a little for by this so much would the Heathen men be shortened of days to ravage the country and make waste of His temples of worship and bring ruin to His abbeys and churches.

Going into his wife Elswitha's chamber after one such talking with Justus, he kissed her fondly and then stood over the cot where his infant son Edward lay wide-eyed and far from sleep.

Elswitha said, "My lord—your face carries a cloud?"

"Aye—but who would have a run of days that were always cloud free? My son is well?"

"Yes, my lord. And full of merry spirit."

"I give thanks for that. And for you—I am gifted to have such a wife. And such healthy son. Two joys which if times were good would be all any man could ask of God."

Justus, at that same time, was sitting on a bench with Paternus outside his lodge, beakers of ale at their side while Paternus's wife and Helburga were in the house preparing supper.

Paternus said, "So you badger the king still for your ships?"

"Aye—but it is uphill work."

Paternus laughed. "That is the nature of all work. Maybe, too, it is the nature of all men's lives. Did you hear that some while ago the good mason Arnulf fell to his death from Sherborne roof?"

"Aye, but only a few days ago from a priest of Athelney who waited for audience with the king after me. He was good man and may his soul find peace. Does Helburga know?"

"Aye—for some long time, I think, if I read her right. Does any longing remain with you in that direction?"

"Nay. I have good wife and reach for naught else. Riada stands with ample dowry and being of good sense she will marry some other."

"Good words—and no more on that to be said."

Paternus sighed. "But much on other things. Wessex stands more or less peaceful now and my sword arm aches for true work. But bad times will come again—that you know. For now the Danes build up and hold what they have elsewhere—but when they do come it will be no sudden summer flash storm and flood. God grant me the years to see it and meet it even though my beard be grown grey."

That night as Justus lay abed with Helburga after love-making, he said, "I speak this now and so would have it finished. I know of the death of Arnulf and that Riada has gone back to her people. But except for sadness at her loss I am not with her. I am here with you. And that stands. I see now that in his time a man lives through many lives. That one is passed."

"Even though I yet give you no child?"

"Even though. But hope is a sturdy growth. So no more. If you wish we could take some other woman's babe to be our own."

Helburga turned and put her arms round him, kissed his cheek and said, "Let us give hope longer span to run. And I will make special prayers—aye, and perhaps a little more sharply—to the Holy Mother."

"There is no need. Keep them gentle. She knows all."

*   *   *   *

So the years passed while the Heathen Army tightened its grasp on all the lands to the north of Wessex and not one Wessex man was idle minded enough to think that his country's turn would not come. Between 873 and 875 the Heathen host moved as it wished through all the lands north of London and the Thames, and now it was split into two armies, one under Halfdan which went north to the lands about the river Tyne, and the other led by King Guthrum which deposed King Burghred of Mercia and set up in his place a thane of little worth called Ceolwulf to hold the land for them until such time as they wished to have settled posses-sion of it. This so because there was no Heathen leader among them who did not know that their armies must be kept together in full war state until the day came when they could turn confidently against Wessex and overrun it and make it theirs.

Oricson, a fully seasoned warrior, was now one of the men who stood close to Guthrum, served in his royal war band and had grown a little pompous and proud that he, the son of an almost unknown warrior of Gerskat, should now be close to Guthrum's ear, his service and loyalty marked and his future brightening with the rising knowledge that when the Wessexmen were overrun he would have his pick of lands and cattle ... Aye, and if he so wished when that day came, the pick of some thane's or alderman's daughter for wife as a right of conquest. Not that this when it should happen would take him from Ina. The fen woman had become part of his life and took no heed that he would never take her for wife for she came from a loose community where the Christian ethic was suborned to the harsh demands of each uncertain day and where the priests themselves had their doxies and put pleasure before their duty to God and their community. Aye, a rich Saxon alderman's daughter—and a great slice of his lands, and when family life and wifely scolds irked him the brown-skinned, dark-haired Ina's passion to tease him from his boredom. And, if she by some miracle, bore him children he would find good place for them. Gerskat, he knew, would never be likely to see him again. This country was becoming his place. The thought of the marshman, Justus, seldom now touched his mind—and when it did he could smile and dismiss it. Young blood—quick words. But now he was man, and steadfastly nursed a man's dreams. So, he moved with each season's campaigns with Ina following him, yet—with so many others—his thoughts were always turning southwards, his body sometimes aching with the longing for the day when Guthrum and his army should turn towards Wessex and its conquering.

In those years Justus went steadily on with his work at the shipyards along the southern coasts and during the good seasons Helburga rode with him. Now, he no longer made any complaint to King Alfred when his orders were thwarted. Men could be bent only so far from their traditional ways. He learned to accept with good grace ingrained opposition to change, and longed to meet some man in the yards who would have the imagination and foresight of a Noth, yet found none.

In the summer of 875 he rode with the king and his body-guard from Winchester to Hampton where there lay four ships, newly launched and fitted out and waiting the royal visit. They were all fully crewed and manned with fighting men and Alfred went aboard the flagship with Justus and the royal guard. They sailed on a cross wind to far off the eastern point of the Isle of Wight, a light haze overhanging the sea. Here the fleet commander mounted a demonstration for the king. One ship was appointed to be a heathen craft and the king's ship its attacker, and the whole display went with a smoothness which delighted Alfred. The enemy was over-hauled and as the king's craft moved in the bowmen loosed a cloud of blunt-headed arrows to fall deliberately short of the other ship. As the ships closed, grappling irons were thrown to bring the two together and the enemy ship was boarded and the fighting crews shouted and laughed and swore cheerfully as they made a great show for their king.

But a little later as the small fleet was going through a series of movements, sailing in line ahead and then in line abreast to the command of signal flags hoisted to the mast top of the king's ship—a device which had come from Justus—and individual ships being sent out on side or ahead as lookouts because of the mist, the mock battle moves were suddenly turned to true shape.

From the now fast-rising haze ahead of them there suddenly appeared a handful of dragon ships, no doubt long at sea on their raven's wind pirating and seeking some undefended haven or beaching place to plunder and rewater their hog-skins.

Then did Justus, arrogant of his own skills, long to have command of the Saxon boats, but King Alfred being with them there could only be one commander and no question of his right to call the battle orders that would send the signal flags running to the mastheads.

They closed head on with the dragon ships. The result was confusion though not disgrace. The two small fleets sailed through one another and javelins and arrows, no longer mock ones, flew between them, and from the king's ship—more by luck than skill—three grappling lines were heaved across one of the ships and they closed in brief and bloody battle. But the raven's wind men were unmettled and weary with long sea-days and, although they fought with all the fury they could command, they were overcome and the ship boarded and taken as prize—and this the only prize for the others turned away under sail and oars and with the following wind soon disappeared into the mist.

Late that night, while the merrymaking and celebrations went on at Hampton, Justus was called to the king's lodging where he found Alfred reading his missal by the light of the fire and the draught-blown, guttering candles. The king ignored him for a while, and then turned and looked up at him, his face plain, giving no hint of his mood. For sometime he held Justus's eyes and then suddenly smiled and giving a short laugh said, "Now, good master Justus—read me the lesson which is writ all over your face."

"May I read it frankly, my lord?"

"I want none other."

"Then I say God has given us a small victory—but a heartening one. And the noise of it will travel all the land. But if we had sat war-horses and fought on land we should have had a great victory, for all our men understand such fighting. So now, I say again, we must have men who are sea warriors and know all its skills, and men who stay with and live on or close to their craft. The men and ships we fought were those who still follow the raven's wind on their own. Their ships were battered and some under-manned by long pirating. They knew their power and knew it was not enough to outface us so close to our own shores. There, too, should be sea fyrds as there are land fyrds. How long, my lord, does it take to make a good warrior?"

"You know that answer. Years—and God's protection to grant those years. But years, my good Justus, are not to be granted. So we must be content with what we have." He paused, his face suddenly growing severe, almost bad-tempered, and then went on, "You think we have gained little this day?"

"No, my lord. We have had great gain—because all across your Wessex lands and beyond the story will run—and grow."

Alfred smiled. "I like that last wag of the tail. Aye, it will grow, and with each telling grow more. And so, give all our people fresh heart. And the Heathen food for thought. To you I will say frankly—we made a pig's mess of it. But the reward remains—from now on the Heathens will know that we arm our coasts. So they will not come lightly to us, like wanton boys to raid an idle, drunken man's orchard. Time, Justus—time is the master. And you are its servant more than mine. But be not so truthful with others as you always are with me. Tell the story in bright colours. Boast a little—it puts heart into the doubtful and fires the arrogant. You carry my jewel warrant still—make of it a club, but over-bully no one. Men come to hand with reasoning. And—to send you happy to your couch, remember this—it was a great victory for men's mouths will make it so in the telling and now the Heathen will stand off and hesitate before he turns any headland to sack village or port. God has sent us a poor little victory in which we must have the grace to see the greater ones waiting in time if we keep true trust in Him and by His commandments hold fast to our faith against the Heathens. Now, go make merry with your shipmen, measure not your wine drinking, boast and sing with them. You and I have wise heads on our shoulders—but we must not be above playing children's games when it serves us."

"My lord, you are full of wisdom and I am chastened."

Alfred laughed. "The wisdom I accept since I take pleasure in praise. Your chastening . . . aye, that too I accept. But do not make great show of it to others. Now, as you go, send me in my scholar monk. I begin to get my tongue around his Latin —and when God sends our full meed of peace to this land I would have it in reach of all those who yearn for it as I do. Go and be merry."

Which Justus did—for the truth in his king's words was plain to him.

*   *   *   *

159

Throughout all these years Riada lived in the marshlands and worked when she was needed for the thane's wife. At odd times she had news of Justus. Sometimes from one of the local fyrd men coming back from his tour of duty in the king's army and sometimes from some passing pedlar or packman bringing news of the affairs of Wessex ... news which travelled slowly and in the travelling often grew distorted so that she had an over-coloured picture of Justus. That he had become a great man at the king's side. That he had built a fleet which would chase the Heathens from the seas. That he was married and had no children which made her sad for him, though in his grand new life perhaps that was no lack since his days must be filled with matters that left him little time for family affairs. Sometimes she walked the marsh ways to the dune beach from which Justus had been taken and sat for a while thinking about him and there, free of her children, she had no need to school her emotions and, indeed, found that the solace of weeping for the losses life had brought her emptied her of self-pity and took her back to her everyday life with a new lift in her spirits. But never so great that it moved her towards other men—of whom there were plenty who would have taken her for wife or for passing pleasure. She had given her body and her love to two men. Now the need for such gifting had gone from her.

Oricson, too, had learned that Justus was alive for King Guthrum, though not ready yet to turn finally towards Wessex, kept men there to make report of the state of the Wessex forces and the doings of King Alfred. In attendance on Guthrum one day while riding back from hunting the king said to him, "You are from Gerskat?"

"Aye, my lord."

"I have heard a strange story that these ships the Wessex king builds against us are mastered by one named Justus who was once slave in Gerskat where he learned his craft from one Noth."

"That he was at Gerskat is true, my lord. Though I had thought him long dead—since he escaped in a small craft he built himself."

"He lives by some miracle."

"Aye—miracle it must be. But I am glad for that—since death is sworn between us for an insult passed, but we hold also a backward friendship for he helped me escape my father's will to keep me with him and from this land."

"You would know him if you saw him now?"

Oricson laughed. "Put a beard on him, chop off an arm, blacken his face with charcoal ... aye, I would know him and he would know me, though I now have a beard. The gods have marked us."

Guthrum was silent for a while and then he laughed gently. "Perhaps the gods have put you in my hands. You would serve me without question, and rid me of him?"

"I would my lord—but it must be openly, equal armed."

"I care not for which way you choose. The Saxon Alfred seeks to find means to deny us the seas of his coast. I would have the man go. Aye, small beginning it may be—the sea victory they gained off Wight. But great oaks from little acorns grow. I mean to have Wessex—so, I charge you. Turn trader, Frankish monk, any shape you wish—and go take this man from the Saxon Alfred. The day is soon coming when I need the seas free to passage for more than dragon ship harriers who work on their own small ventures. My steward will give you a list of people you can trust in the Saxon lands and they will know this gage when they see it."

As he spoke he unpinned from his blue cambric short summer cloak a circular gold brooch worked with a design of four intertwined gripping beasts. He handed it to Oricson, saying, "This all those who work for me in the Saxon lands will know for they hold brooches like this. Go and do this work for me. And when you return I promise you that you shall stand at my right hand in battle and shall have when the day comes your pick of good Saxon lands."

So a few days later Oricson with Ina rode south to London, which the Heathens still held firmly, and there from the power of his secret writ from Guthrum made a compact with a Frankish merchant who was travelling west with a mule string carrying his wares. War or its threat might hang over the land, but the ways of traders were ever open no matter the risks they took. Oricson rode as a bodyguard with two other men and, since the merchant travelled his wife with him, Ina joined herself to this lady's service. To all questions from her for the reason of this change in Oricson's way of life he gave no direct answer, but smiled and said, "When it is time for you to know, you shall know, but for now be content and the time will come when merchants shall enter bowing to your boudoir and open their bales for you to take your pick of their fine silks and jewellery."

A few days later they rode west along the south bank of the Thames and then took the broken old Roman road along the northern side of the great Wealden forests that ran as far as the eyes could reach. Dressed now no longer as a warrior, Oricson wore woollen trews, a leather jerkin, a short cloak, and hanging from his belt a plain but well-honed sword. Alongside him at the head of the train the trader looked at him and smiled, saying, "One thing remember, Guthrum man—when you come to your real business do me the courtesy of carrying it out far from my sight and out of my knowledge. I am as honest as a trader can be in these days and would rather have ignorance in my mind than lies on my lips."

Oricson smiled. "Never fear. 'Twill be done and when it is done you shall only know it by my leaving you. It gives me no pleasure to wear a near packman's garb."

The trader grunted and shrugged his shoulders, saying, "You warriors conquer by the sword—but since time began there has always been a greater conquest made by my kind."

"Maybe, but having made it, you need us for its keeping."

6

TWO MONTHS LATER in the early Autumn of 875 when
the Heathen kings, Guthrum, Oscytel and Osmund were with
their forces gathered at Cambridge into winter quarters,
Oricson came for the second time to Winchester in search of
Justus. He had travelled as far west as Exeter and Athelney
in his quest and was often irked by the slowness of the
merchant's movements since the man would turn aside to the
smallest hamlet for chance of trading but Oricson had the
wisdom to know he must stand by him to be unmarked as
would have been a single armed man. The thing to be done
had to be done openly and yet without witnesses. He was no
assassin to take a man without warning with a dagger into his
back. Here, in a tavern close to the Southgate where the trader
lodged and made his market, the man came and sat by him
as the daylight faded to show the growing brightness of the
first stars.

He said, "I have news for you. Today I was summoned to
the king's wife, the Lady Elswitha, to show her my wares. She
sat with her maid, a saucy piece who quipped and joked with
her and made her laugh and wrapped my lengths of silk
and velvet about her body to display them for her lady. And
while she did this the king himself with a bearded, well-set
young attendant came in and the maid, teased and spurred on
by them, made a dancing show and all was good-humoured
and a little saucy—"

"You make a long tale of this."

"It runs longer—and to your end. Afterwards the maid
took me into the servants' hall to be given ale and to wait
until payment for my goods was brought to me. However,

though money and trading is my first concern, I have that other which serves your King Guthrum well so I asked her about the king's movements lately and also enquired the standing of the man with him. It was your shipwright, Justus, who now that his work runs more smoothly, returns often to the king's side and is with his royal guard again."

Oricson's hands firmed around the beaker he held and said, "Tell me of him and where he is to be found?"

"He is married and lives not far from the Southgate in a small lodge that fronts the river. It is easily found for it stands alone close to the great hill that looks over the river. You should know it for at the foot of the garden is moored a small boat which he has made for his wife's pleasure. The place stands well enough on its own for your business— though when it be done, make no return to me." He grinned and blew out his lips. "I am honest trader in the world's eyes."

The next evening, as the westering sun began to throw long shadows over the river valley, Oricson, long-cloaked to hide the sword that hung from his belt, walked to the river, found the house and hid himself in a clump of osiers at the bottom of the garden by the water's edge. Justus, he had learned, was on guard duty until sunset. Near at hand the small boat which Justus had made for his wife was drawn up free from the water. One look at it told him that there could be no other like it on this river. It was of sweet line and smoothly made—Noth marked, he thought.

From the lodge came no light or sound of movement. Swallows and swifts, soon to turn southwards, hawked low over the river. Night moths had already begun to flight above the tall grasses. Now and again there was the sound of a water-rail calling unmusically from upstream. He watched the trout and grayling rising to a sudden hatch of fly. All these things, he thought calmly, were as they once had been on the mere-side at Gerskat ... aye, even to the slow passage over the far willows of a heron, ghosting downstream ... where he had sat often with Justus. For a moment or two he was touched with the brief sadness of the fate which linked him with Justus. The gods had tossed a game dice with only two markings—

one for friend and one for foe. It could so easily have fallen for friend—and now he almost wished it had ... would have, had he not hastily spoken the insult of marsh-girls' scaly backsides. He laughed inwardly to himself at the irony. And double irony ... for had he not lost his heart to one of these same marsh girls? And, by Frey and Freya, he would stand on oath and swear that her backside was as round as an apple and as smooth as the smoothest spread of fine silk ...

The first of the pipistrelle bats began to drop down from the thatched roof of the lodge for their evening's hawkings and as they did so he heard the sound of someone coming down the river path. A man passed within feet of his hiding place, and he saw clearly that it was Justus, but a Justus now who had grown to manhood and carried himself with unconscious pride ... aye, which he could for the jump from marshman to the king's shipwright was in its way like one of the fairy stories his mother had told him of spelled frog turning into high-born prince.

He let him pass and saw him pause by the moored boat and check the knot of the painter which held it to its mooring stake. Noth would have done that, and so now did Noth's shadow. Oricson moved forward a little in his hiding place.

Justus turned then and came back along his path until he stood a spear's length from the tree clump which hid Oricson. Then, in an even voice, Justus said, his hand on the hilt of his sword, "Come from there. You stirred as I passed and the last of the sun took the light from your sword mount."

Oricson was still for a moment or two, and then he laughed and stepped from his hiding place into the evening light, both his hands raised, free from sword and belt dagger. Keeping his distance, he said, "So after all these years the gods bring us together, marshman. As we both have always known they would. You know me?"

Justus looked at his bearded face and down the run of his armed body and said, "I should because something stirs in me. But one thing I know is that you are not true Saxon for that tells in your speech—though you speak it as well as many a well-tongued stranger."

Oricson gave a little laugh. "Nor would I have known you at first sight. Though as I face you now much of the old Justus comes to life. To goad your memory a little, shall I give you an old question which lies between us and yet needs your answer?"

"Aye, do that. My life has been full of questions asked— and many never truly answered."

"Then take this one again. I asked you once whether the girls in your marshlands had scales on their backsides. And you promised me answer in kind if we should ever meet as both free men."

Justus was silent for a while, and then he smiled.

"Aye, so I did. And now it all comes back. But since long years have passed, and I have good memories of your father and of Noth and am good Christian myself, I say to you—go without my answer."

"Aye—there would be sense in that. We were young. But I swore an oath which cannot be taken back. The words you kept to yourself then are now fallen due to me—and I would have them."

"So be it since you ask it. When you made rude jest of marsh girls—I would have replied in kind. I give you the words now. Is it true that when the raven's wind men go voyaging that the lust in their wives is so strong that their sons at home service their mothers?"

Oricson laughed quietly. "By Odin—'tis nothing like so strong as I thought to hear ... aye, and may have truth in it, but 'twill serve."

"Then do me a kindness before I kill you. My wife is within the lodge. Move up the bank a little where there is a fall of water the sound of which will cover our sword noise."

"For you—I make it a last kindness ... aye, and now I come to think of it, maybe the first. See, I go ahead with my back to you for I know you are a man of honour."

So they moved upstream a little to the side of the river fall into a large mill pool.

In the lodge Helburga lay on the bed in the loft above the main room. The window was unshuttered to the riverside garden. She had lain content while Oricson had taken his place in the willows, her mind bland with a now even-paced joy. During all her years with Justus she had with waning hope notched her courses stick to mark the days between them, though now she kept this secret from Justus since the hope in her was worn thin. But this day, and she gave praise to God for it, she had for the third time in a week been as sick as a dog, and that a sickness which had not come from tainted food for her stick was notched to show that she was well overdue of her woman's sickness. But not once had she given by word or look any sign of her growing happiness to Justus for she would be certain before she spoke. No doubt lingered in her now and as she lay she pressed her two breasts and fancied they already began to swell with the coming milk ...

To whom did he talk in the garden? Though nothing strange in that since men of affairs and the royal guard and shipwrights from near Swanage and Hampton often journeyed to see him ... He was important man, and carried the king's jewel warrant ... a thing she often held and turned to fire or sunlight to see the blaze of brilliant colours. Knowing that Justus travelled rough at times she always wrapped it for him in a doe-skin pouch stuffed with swansdown ... Aye, and polished the golden beast head and the gold chasing on the back plates with their elaborate tree scrolls and basket work designs. Pride for Justus was sometimes like a fire in her blood, and when they lay in consort the fire moved into her flesh and skin to make a passion heat between them that often left her afterwards shaking and weeping for joy. Joy was now soon to be double joy for she knew his longing for a child ... above all for a son but for that grace there was nought to be done but to wait on God's goodness.

Now he talked in the garden with someone, light friendly talk with a laugh now and then for most men liked him. She smiled to herself—unless he were thwarted, which he was less so now than in the early days. She lay still and schooled her impatience. She would pour him the Frankish wine which she had bought in the market this day, and serve him the thing he loved best ... she giggled to herself ... being a marsh and

167

sea man ... a wine-sauced dish of sole with a red-pink chaplet of large prawns to edge his platter and she would let him eat and drink first and when he was done and he asked her for the news of her day—she would tell him ...

She sat up from her bed then for sounds had suddenly come to her ... sounds to which she was no stranger for many a time she had watched Paternus and his guards on the palace yard going through their sword drills, and had heard and seen the real thing when in the early days journeying with Justus and good, well-armed merchant company she had stood within the cart circle and watched a hungry desperate band of vagabonds and outlaws try—though with short-lived determination—to take and pillage the baggage train. Then, suddenly, she heard Justus laugh long and loud above the clashing ring of sword music. She rose from the bed couch and went swiftly backwards down the loft ladder and out into the garden. Looking up stream she saw the two men fighting a little below the mill pool. She screamed and began to run towards them.

Neither man heard her scream, nor saw her running. They were held in the dark circle of sword and blood trance, knowing nothing of the world around them. They saw only the other's face, the battle crouch of his body, the man to be killed, and heard nothing but the stamp of their feet, the harsh whistle of their breathing as sword swung and was taken on like sword blade. The world of the calm evening with the first stars finding dim light above, and the rich outpouring of thrush and high set lark dropping to ground, was lost to them.

For Justus there was only Oricson, and for Oricson only Justus, and for thought there was none. For them lived only sword arm, sword thrust, the moving, crouching, menacing shape that danced and jumped and sweated and grunted before them, and the parry of sword by sword, and the grunt of breath lost and breath taken, and the stamp of feet on the river grasses and herbs and the ecstasy which takes even the vilest of fighting men as the lust for killing runs through them like a fever-fire.

As she neared the two men Helburga screamed again and this time Justus heard her and glanced quickly back over his shoulder even as he raised his sword arm to parry a thrust from

Oricson. But the force of the blow and part turn of his body towards Helburga rocked him off balance and he stumbled backwards and fell to his knees. Oricson laughed and swung his blade in a wide half-circle to slash the exposed side of Justus's neck. But the blow never fell for Helburga came between them and, with a wild cry of terror, caught at his arm with both hands and unsteadied the blow so that the great blade swept high over Justus's head. Then, hardly knowing what he did, caught up in the fighting lust and maddened by the woman who clung to his sword arm Oricson swung his dagger arm sideways and plunged the blade into her breast. She groaned high and long and then fell back on the grass at Justus's feet as he came up from the ground, seized suddenly with a blacker and bloodier passion than he had ever known in his life. He leaped over Helburga's body and under the high-raised sword of Oricson and kicked him with wild fury between the legs in his crotch.

Oricson's body jerked backwards, his mouth gaping with the pain in his groin, and his raised sword swung wide. Its weight took him out of control and his body swayed forward. Justus saw the nape of his head and the brown skin of his exposed neck and slashed his sword down. As the blade bit deep he heard the man's high moan of death agony suddenly choke and die as the blood spouted from the wound, black in the fading light. Then Oricson fell face forward on the trampled grass to lie close to Helburga. For a moment or two his body jerked and twitched in the closing death grip and then was still. They lay together. Helburga with her face turned to the now fast darkening sky, the stars taking growing light from the oncoming darkness, and Oricson with his face hidden in the trampled grasses, his arms outflung, the spread fingers of his now weaponless hands twitching for a moment or two, grasping at the earth, seeking to hold the world he knew but to which he now could no longer make claim.

Beyond him Justus knelt and gathered Helburga to him, holding and cradling her in his arms, kissing her warm face and cajoling and whispering to her. She lay still in his arms as though in deep sleep, and there was a cold despair in Justus's heart that seized him like hardening frost.

He took her in his arms gently and rose and carried her back to the lodge and to her bed, and he bound and staunched her death wound and bathed her body clean and gave her fresh gown and then ribboned back her fair hair. Kneeling at her side he made his own prayers for her soul, and so stayed all night in vigil. When the dawn came, he left the lodge and carried the news to Paternus and her sister.

Two days later he was summoned to the king's presence where, to his surprise and to his honour, Alfred for a moment or two put his hands on his shoulders and pressed him to his breast and then said gently, "I seek no words for there are none that fit such sorrow. In time God will give you comfort. For myself I will give you anything you ask for you have served me well. Say what is in your mind."

Justus was silent for a while, and then he said, "My lord, I would serve you still as ship-master, but we both know that that is slow growth which will, with God's goodness, fruit beyond our times. Yet will I serve you in that way until the day comes which already you see ahead when the Heathens will return in force. Then would I have right from you to take my place with the royal bodyguard at your side and do battle with the Heathen. I ask no more than that and, if God wills it, to die in your service."

"The right is yours, Justus."

*   *   *   *

The news of Helburga's death and Justus's sorrow came to Riada a few days before Candlemas in the following year, 876. It was given to her by a young yeoman on his return to Athelney after duty in the winter fyrd of King Alfred. He was one of many who would have courted her had she shown wish. But there was no fire or turn in her towards any man. Two losses she had suffered, first Justus and then good Arnulf. Both had gifted her with children—and these now claimed all her love and grew each in his way to the shaping of their fathers, though being boys they could act like hell hounds when the wind set in the right quarter and then took as fair due a whipping of their backsides with a stout withy stick.

The day she had the news, she walked the frost-bound iron-hard marsh paths by the side of the frozen meres and channels to the long dune beach where so many years ago Justus had been taken from her. The cold wind whipped at the folds of the great cloak she wore and its bite brought tears to her eyes to which were joined the tears of her true sorrows. Blown wave-spume raced across the sands, flocks of dunlin foraged the water's edge and shelduck and greenshanks worked the sand flats as the tide drew back. She stood for a long time facing the sea, weeping. Then she turned away and going to the dunes passed the place where her love and Justus's had been joined. Going back across the dunes she stopped under the clump of wind-twisted crab apple trees and reached up and plucked one lone surviving apple from its bare branches. It was as cold as a beach stone, and when she bit into it the flesh was hard and sour. For a moment she moved to throw it away and then, without knowing why except that the need had risen suddenly in her, she walked on and ate the whole fruit.

Long before this Ina, in her London lodging, had the news of Oricson's death from his friend Weyn who had come from King Guthrum's winter quarters at Cambridge as guard captain to a merchant baggage train.

She took the news calmly for it was not in her fen nature to show her true emotions openly. Loss was something you took and held and carried to some place of quiet and isolation before you gave it full rein.

Weyn said, "He died in fair fight with his Justus—though the gods could not deny themselves a little unexpected mischief for Justus's wife was killed as she tried to come between them."

"A little of my weeping shall be for her."

"So now—you are without man and a child to be for that shows clearly. What would you do?"

"That which is in your mind—for I read you as a good man ... and, aye in truth, only my love for Oricson stood between your wanting and my offering. But now there is brat to come of mixed blood and many more such mixings there will be all over this country."

"That way is blood strengthened often. But I will be honest. You need protector. I was close friend to Oricson. I will, if you say the word, take you back to Cambridge and lodge you safely there for all the country is ours. Here, by yourself, as soon as your body were free of the babe some pander would trap you. Will you come?"

"You will stand in Oricson's place as father to the child?"

Weyn laughed and laid the back of his hand gently against her sun-browned cheek. "Aye—and to the others that must surely follow. Oricson had a dream ... to take land here and become one with this country. That now is the fever in the blood of all raven's wind men. I hold that dream, too. Together we shall see it come true and through our children see the joining of my country with yours ... though, by Odin, I pray that the settling comes not too soon for I am still young and eager for sword work to bring me land and contentment in the far years when I can ride gently out on an autumn morning to hawk for partridges among the corn stubble without fear of sudden strife. So, woman—gather up your chattels, and I will find cart for you and ride guard with my men over you back to Guthrum's camp."

*   *   *   *

Later, in that year of 876, the Heathen host marched swiftly out of Cambridge and descended on Wessex with a suddenness that found the Saxons unprepared. They rode swiftly across the land to the southern coast and took the sea-port stronghold of Wareham in Dorset. King Alfred and his fyrds besieged them there and a parley was held by which it was agreed that the Danes should pass hostages of rank to the king and then with their army leave his lands. All this they swore on the holy relics Alfred placed before them and also on their Woden-born rings.

But within a few days the Heathens broke their truce and, breaking out suddenly one night, rode mounted through the Saxon camp, killed all who stood in their way, slaughtered the Saxon warriors' horses as they were hobbled in pasture close to King Alfred's battle camp, and then rode free to the westward safe from present pursuit. In a few days they were at Exeter on the east bank of the river Exe and there threw up and manned that city's defences with such stoutness that none could come at them. They harried the countryside around and in a short while were provisioned with cattle, reaped the harvest crops and then settled down to pass the winter there and to wait for the arrival of an army of their brother kind to cross the waters from Frankland and join them.

King Alfred, camped with his besieging forces before Exeter, sat in council in a monastery barn and spoke firm and hard to the aldermen and thanes who had gathered with their fyrd men. Knowing that treachery now might strike from any point, or any hand long thought loyal—since loyalty changes easily for some with hard times—the king moved nowhere without his royal guard. So it was that Justus and Paternus heard him speak in the dust-filled air of the barn while the sparrows that nested high in the rafters flew in and out of the open windows and panicked and called in alarm at the stir below them.

The talk was hard and bitter. This was the beginning, long foreseen. The Heathen now would raid and raid, here and there with sharp suddenness. And others, as now in Exeter, would sit them down to bear siege and wait for more of their kind to arrive from Frankland by sea and from Mercia and Northumbria. The first of the true days of the destiny of Wessex had arrived. Sharply and angrily he spoke—and though he still lacked three years of reaching his thirty—it was a voice hardened with bitterly come maturity and harder found wisdom of men and their affairs. When he had given all men the tale of the future he called forth his chaplain monk and every man bent the knee as the good man offered up prayer to the Almighty for the safety of all Wessex and its House of Cerdic king.

When the gathering had gone the king sat on an upturned ale tun and sank his chin into his cupped hands and was silent for a while. Paternus and Justus flanked him, armed and still, both knowing that in this moment an even greater distance lay between them and their lord for he was beset by troubles and foreknowledge that come to few men. Then, suddenly, he raised his head and laughed aloud, ran the fingers of a hand through his fair hair, tugged his beard to tidiness, and said, "Was it strong and bodied enough, Justus?"

"Aye, my lord. Far more so than any ale that ever came out of the tun you sit on."

"And will touch them, Paternus? Hold them to me and this country for I fancy it is the will of God that we shall have to bear sharp chastisement in the coming seasons?"

"It will hold them, my lord, for this time there is no place in the whole of this land where any man can turn his back on a near neighbour's distress. They come this time with a wide harrow that reaches from our southern seas to Mercia and beyond."

The king smiled. "Rough-tongued Paternus ... you begin to take some of Justus's easy flowing words. But you speak truth." Then looking at Justus, he went on. "You have faith in your ship captains."

"Aye, my lord."

"You would be with them—for you know there is hard-bound word that a Heathen fleet is ready to make passage from Frankland?"

"This I know my lord. And I have faith in them. They know their part. But—"

"You bite off on a small word. Give me your but."

"I would be with them, my lord, if a fleet should try the crossing from Frankland to join the Heathen here."

Alfred smiled and scratched his bearded chin. "Aye, and so you should be there and shall stand in my stead." He sighed. "And now I would have you leave me and stand guard outside. But keep me in sight. Black days soon stain some men's loyalty."

And black days they were, and days that grew from weeks, to months to years, and the whole of the lands of Wessex was unsettled and there was little peace for men to seed and reap their yardlands to harvest. With some men of Wessex, who should have been first in rank and standing to stay by the king's side, there was a falling away from their loyalty for they looked now ahead to the craven wisdom of changing it and bowing the knee to the Heathens as their hold on the country grew slowly bolder and stronger. But where God sends black days to test the faith of weak men, so He sent—like sudden sun shafts through dark clouds—days of hope to cheer those who held their spirits firm and found no wavering in their trust that under His guidance the days of defeat would turn to victory for them.

In the autumn of 877 the expected Heathen fleet appeared off the south coast and here they were met by Justus and his new formed fleet, and each ship manned with crew and warriors long drilled and trained by his orders and overlooking. As a conceit to hearten his sea command the great square sail of the leading craft he had had dyed and painted in the shape and colouring of the king's jewel which he carried always as his sign of authority under the Cerdic Alfred. Leading the line of battle, the great sail full with a following wind, the ship bore down on the Heathens, the sun striking with midday blaze on the rich jewel colours and the encircling words—*Alfred had me made.*

The battle was short but bloody, and the Heathen fleet— already weary with a hard weather crossing, though this day the sun blazed from a cloudless sky—was broken and many craft fired to destruction by the flinging of blazing brands so that in the end the enemy turned away to save what could be saved and the victory went to the Saxons. It was a victory sore needed to put heart into them. Leaving the fleet then, Justus rode to give the news of the battle to King Alfred. But there was little news of the king's whereabouts … rumours a-plenty, but sound truth short. He was at Winchester, at Wimborne, he held a line of the Thames close to Reading … each man had a different tale. But with hard riding and iron-lying at nights Justus finally found him in his own marshlands, lodged with his royal guard troops and a handful of stout-hearted aldermen and thanes close to Athelney. And since his men slept rough and many under the open sky the king had lodged himself in the hut of a simple cowherd.

When Justus went in to him the king rose and embraced him and then said, " 'Tis pity you arrived not a few minutes earlier. For as I sat here, brooding on the perils of this land, the good cowherd's wife charged me to keep an eye on the oat cakes she had set on the fire griddle while she went for fresh wood to fuel it. Sadly, I let them burn and so was roundly scolded as my good wife Elswitha sometimes scolds me for playing too rough with my son or raising muddy riding boots to her day couch when I would fling myself down, weary to rest. So must any true king accept rebuke from a loyal subject." He handed the still half filled beaker of poor beer he held for Justus to take and went on, "Drink, for I can see you have ridden far and long."

"Aye, my lord. But bring good news."

"Rumours a-plenty I have had. It is true then?"

"God's truth, my lord. And God's hand behind it."

So he sat crouching over the fire with his king and gave him an account of the battle victory of the fleet, and finished, "Now our ships keep station along the coast under a good commander and I doubt that any Heathen fleet will try the sea ways with light hearts."

"You have served me well."

"And would serve you now in that place which you first found for me." He reached within the breast of his long cloak and took out the king's jewel and handed it to Alfred, saying, "I have taken good care of it, but from hard riding and lying the stick pointer worked loose and became lost. I will fashion you another, my lord."

"Aye, and so you shall, but that is a courtesy I make no claim to until better times. Go find Paternus and join his guard—you will get rough but warm greeting for many of his guard will never draw sword again."

After Justus had left the king sat fingering the jewel for a while and then slipped it into the worn pouch on his sword belt. Two days later, while riding through the Athelney thickets, the sharp spur of a broken alder branch caught at the loose pouch flap and tore it part free. When, later, King

Alfred dismounted in a muddy clearing to meet with the thanes and yeoman who were gathering to his side, the jewel fell unnoticed to the ground and was soon foot-and-hoof-trampled into the mud and mire of the marshland mount of Athelney. Its loss was to go unmarked by the king for many weeks and then, when discovered, to be of little concern to him for his mind was too full of greater matters. For now and to run for months to come there grew an awakening in the land, a rising of spirit from despair, and a new boldness of body and fierce lust to deny all the might of the Heathen forces which rode and harried Wessex at will. So men turn un-expectedly in times of darkest peril lusting to hazard them-selves to the impossible and to find—if God so will it—honourable death rather than craven living. Better the body should perish taking with it an unbroken spirit and faith than that the neck should be bowed to accept the overlordship of heathen men and heathen gods. And in those days and the days to come there was no man of true worth and courage who held higher hope in his mind than to die in faith for the safe-guarding of his homeland.

* * * *

Some days after the king's small army had left Athelney Riada's father, the thane's huntsman, came to her where she worked at the weaving loom in the quarters of the thane's wife. Finding her alone, he spoke frankly.

"The king and his men have gone—and Justus with them."

"Aye, I know."

"Did you have word with him?"

"For what reason should I? He now stands high above me."

"You would let him run—knowing he has son by you?"

"Father, it is all time passed and too many doors have been opened and closed. If he thinks to wed again he will not look this way. Father, you mean well, but your arrow falls short of the butt. I am content and have peace here with my child-ren."

"Yet no protection. There is one you know who would give you that ... a good yeoman."

Riada shook her head. "Some news comes late to you. He has ridden with the king, too."

"And taken no promise from you?"

"He is too good a man to wish that and so put greater burden on me that he may never return. You, yourself, would have ridden, too, but for the thane putting all here under your protection."

"Aye ... and little enough and feeble is that. But you will have him on his return?"

"I know not. If he comes on a fine day ... maybe, yes. But if on another full of old memories ... then maybe not. You ask too much of me father in the way of foreknowledge. The one thing I know is that if Justus had wanted me he would have sought me out."

"In God's name, woman. What man goes a wooing only on a fine day? He has long over-passed you and forgotten you."

"Then so be it. I have his son and that of Arnulf—and times are when I find in the favouring of one over the other because of its fathering that I am in fault. I do not wish to add a third chick to my small nest here."

Her father spat angrily to the ground and said coarsely, "Words, words. You are woman. Do you not miss a man beside you on the bed shelf at night?"

Riada laughed. "Oh, yes—for I am woman still. But, father, that is a matter which does not plague a woman so burningly as men believe. You mean kindness, and I take it so. Justus lives in another world. I live in mine. Let it rest that way."

*   *   *   *

In the year of 878 as the weeks moved towards Eastertide there came a change over the ravaged land of Wessex which in after years Alfred was to know sprang from the hand of God. It was as though the warming Spring winds and the fast green leafing and flowering of woods and fields and orchards marked the death of black days and the new birth in Saxon men of

178

a shame at their weakness and lack of faith in the rightness of their cause and a holy rage in their breasts against the Heathens. Without being called men came from far and wide and sought out the king's small and hunted army. They left families and crops to seek and serve him as though God had put a passion in their hearts from which they were fired to work a miracle. King Alfred became the living symbol of Christian hope and faith. None knew the miracle as it came. It touched the lowest man who slept with his master's cattle, stirred placid, self-seeking carls with their ample yardlands, roused thanes who had already laid aside their arms and stood ready to pay tribute to the Heathen and fired earls and aldermen who stood secretly prepared to pay ransom and fat fee for the holding of their lands to the Danes. The fires first of shame and then of patriotism burned through them all, and many a stout monk buckled on belt and sword, said short prayer, and went joyfully to do the Lord's work against the Heathen bands and armies that stood poised to ride with wanton passion to the overthrow of Wessex, the last stronghold of the Saxons to stand against them and that now already ravaged far and wide.

Some weeks after Easter as though at far higher command than King Alfred's a host of fighting men had joined him in Wiltshire west of the town of Chippenham, where the Heathen host had made a stronghold and from which they had long harried the countryside. Riding the guard posts on the night before the day would come—as every man knew—for the joining of battle, war-hardened Paternus turned to Justus at his side with a grin and said, "Did you ever see such a rat swarm of warriors before . . .? God give the king His power to hold and command them when the dawn comes, for holding they need and would even take the field now if let. 'Tis miracle, Justus. Pray God we live to sing the telling of it to those who are but babes in arms now. Aye, and embroider it somewhat."

"You are so sure of victory?"

"Would you have a piece of parchment with the certainty of Holy Writ on it that it shall be so? I say only—if it come not true then hereafter any man of small or great rank can spit in my face and call me coward and I will lift no hand against him. God stands with us. And when He so stands— the holy spirit runs like fire through the blood."

"You should make song of it."

"God grant me the days to do it."

"And me to hear it."

"And know this. We shall have victory and after that others ... aye and maybe a few defeats. But that is only the run of the stream which turns now and then to make a back eddy. But in time the sea is reached. When the saints bless your war banners they do it honestly for they can do no less. And remember this—which is much nearer home—before we join battle tomorrow morning void your bowels and bladder or the battle spasms will do it for you which is a plaguey nuisance when there are no women around to serve at wash-tub for you afterwards. And stay by my side with the king. He is our holy charge and this country needs long years to come from him for when men like him are made the mould is quick broken and only the years can shape such another."

That night King Alfred lay sleepless for a long time in his tent, and he, too, wondered still at the miracle which had brought his army into being, and could only believe that God out of His wisdom sometimes put His children to great trials to rouse them from their worldliness to a new and stronger faith in Him—and was this not, too, the way of a worldly father with his children: to sharpen them with chastisements to turn them from idleness and soft pleasures to know that the only true joy in life lay in service and duty? Pleasures not earned were cheap market wares that gave short comfort.

He slept little that night and was wakened long before dawn with the report that the Heathen warriors had come out from Chippenham and had formed a battle camp on a hilltop some few miles away at Edington to bar the passage of the Wessex forces to their Chippenham stronghold. He rose then, called his priest and made brief prayers, but with no lack of sincerity since he knew that the Lord called him to a duty which held place above all others this day.

Paternus came to him, already helmeted and battle-geared

with byrnie, shield and broad sword, his face beaming with a smile so that Alfred said wryly, "You smile, Paternus, as though this were the day of a country fair for singing and dancing and the tweaking of maidens' bottoms."

"Greater pleasure than that, my lord."

"Why so?"

"Because the Heathens come to meet us."

"Why should they not?"

"Because they cannot hold Chippenham and deny us battle. They seek a quick victory in the open. This is no time of the year to stand siege against us in Chippenham ... 'tis but May time. No crops, no fruits yet ... cattle, aye, yes—but how would they get beasts for slaughter if we penned them up? They have eaten their winter stores ... so they come out for quick victory. True warriors they are—but like all men they carry a traitor in their bellies ... hunger if food is denied them. In a day's riding there are few pickings to find around their Chippenham stronghold."

"So we must win this battle and drive them back to it."

"Aye, my lord. And then starve them into a final quitting of this Wessex land."

"But first we must take victory here at Edington."

"Which we shall and bloody enough it will be for they will fight with a battle madness. Yet we shall match it for we fight not to fill our bellies but to hold under God that which is ours—and already the lowest serf with spear and wooden shield in our ranks knows this. Though ask me not how ... It runs like the kick of strong ale in them."

"God grant that there be truth in your words."

Truth there was. Long afterwards men told the story of that day which was the certain beginning of the end of the Heathen curse on the land though many years would pass before the slow yeast of the future worked to its proper rising. Men may be conquered but not a country. Already the Danes had begun to love and covet the land—and in that lay their own defeat, their own turning from warriorhood to the longer lasting passion of peaceful possession and an intermingling of bloods that would make all give fidelity to one statehood.

The battle at Edington was bloody and since in battle each man knows only his small part of it none could tell the twists and turns of all its hours. Under King Guthrum the Danes held firm for a while, but then their own berserk warriors, eager for blood, broke ranks and charged and the Saxons held them and threw them back. All through that morning and long after noon men fought and men died and the Wessex men held firm under Alfred's strong hand. No man turned a back and ran in the Wessex ranks for each knew that to run would gain nothing. Though few then could have put it into words, all felt within them the rare, disregarding courage of doomsday passion. Before the sun set on that day of destiny the Saxons knew that they would live hereafter either as slaves or freemen. Time and the years ahead meant nothing—this day was paramount, God-ordained. So each in his own way, with the memory of his own patch of land and family, his own broad acres and thane's or alderman's hall, fought with a stronger, steadier passion than any berserk warrior knew.

Justus and Paternus fought at King Alfred's side and clove to him through all the confusion of Heathen charges from their hilltop, and in the last of those charges Justus found himself facing a Danish warrior whose face held a grim but true grin as he took delight in the day's savagery, and though neither knew it of the other, one was Weyn, the friend of Oricson, and the other the killer of that friend. Though their clashing was brief, in their fighting Justus slipped on the blood-soaked turf of the hillside and, as he fell, Weyn slashed his sword and cut him through the upper part of his left thigh until the blade met bone and then overleapt him to meet another Saxon warrior.

And so the battle swung for hours in the balance, and high above the larks sang and the carrion birds, the eagles, kites and ravens, swung in leisurely circles waiting for the time when they could drop to the feast that the warriors below were laying out for them.

In the end the Heathens under their King Guthrum turned away from the fight and swarmed back to the safety of their stronghold at Chippenham, and here the Saxons besieged them, knowing full well that in short time they would be starved into surrender for of all men's masters there is none stronger than the belly which demands to be filled.

Two days later when Paternus came to give King Alfred a full tally of the Saxon losses at Edington, naming by rank and station the dead and wounded, he finished, "And with them lies Justus ... by the grace of God alive."

"Aye, then for that I give thanks for I saw him go down at my side."

"But he will never stand there again as a whole man, my lord, for the sword slash has crippled his left leg. But he lives and will heal."

"And will turn back from warrior to his true work as shipmaster. See that he is well tended. Now give me the tally of the Heathen dead."

*   *   *   *

So in the growing summer days of 878 began the siege of Chippenham and after two weeks the Heathen forces sued for peace and King Guthrum—which no Dane had ever done before—begged for truce and free passage from the Saxon lands, and pledged himself to become a Christian and to take Baptism at the hand of King Alfred. This last no man could ever tell whether it was from true conviction or statesmenlike courtesy. But one truth remained: the West Saxons had freed themselves at last from the Heathen threat of conquest. Promises might be broken and then mended, again and again—but Wessex would stay free and grow in might so that with the coming of the years all the other realms of the land would look towards the Saxons and their kings as the true seat of power and authority in the land. Men with rare wisdom enough to divine it would come to know that in war and conquest there is only one victor and that is the good earth over which battles are fought and which, when the blood letting is done, ever remains to be seeded and cropped with the rhythm of the seasons and that while swords rust from lack of use the share that turns the long furrows for the sowing of corn remains ever bright.

Early that autumn, on the thirteenth Sunday after Trinity, with his left leg well mended, though he limped and used a stout stave to help his walk, Justus rode back to his marshes on his way to Athelney to talk to the king before going on to Exeter and his shipyards. But on his way he turned aside and followed the marsh path down to the long beach from which, so many years past, he had been taken by the men of the *Fafnir*.

He tethered the horse to the wind-twisted crab apple tree and walked through the dunes to the beach. He had sent a messenger ahead of him to his marsh village to speak of the time and place of his coming. He knew that the moment he topped the last dune rise he would know whether he would be welcomed.

Over his head a skein of wild geese flew north to the sea, and low over the waving dune grasses late swallows hawked their south-bound way.

He came out from the last of the dunes on to the sea-wrack strewn lip of the long beach. Away to his left the river ran down to the sea to meet the coming tide. This was the beach where he had lain with his love. Since then there had been other loves, other lives. And now, seeing it empty of human life, he felt that he had been wrong to come. There was no turning back to the past, no reaching out for the joys of years now lost in time.

Then from behind him he heard the sound of feet on the high-tide ridge of pebbles. She came down to him from the path he had followed, a saffron-coloured cloak over her shoulders, the light wind fretting her long flaxen hair across her face, and she stopped a few paces from him and held her arms across her breasts as though she were suddenly cold.

They stood, unspeaking, unmoving. Then suddenly she ran to him and he dropped his stave and took her into his arms. She buried her face in his shoulder and he felt her body shake against him as though she shivered with some long-held cold-ness which only the warmth of his embrace could comfort.

So he held her, without words, without caress, and the gulls

184

cried above them and the long waves behind them ran seething up the beach to fringe it with the light froth of their breaking and the wind took the stranded spume and blew it like thistledown along the sands.